David Thomson

First Yankee

David Thomson: First Yankee
Copyright 2020 by Barbara Newall
On behalf of Seacoast Science Center, Rye, NH

All rights reserved. No part of this book may be reproduced without permission of the author. This edition of David Thomson: First Yankee is based on the original work of Ralph Thomson, and the sketches of Matthew Thomson, both direct descendants of David Thomson.

Published by Piscataqua Press
32 Daniel St., Portsmouth NH 03801
www.piscataquapress.com

ISBN: 978-1-950381-32-6

Printed in the United States of America.

David Thomson
First Yankee

Barbara Newall
Ralph Thomson

Introduction

When his father died, David Thomson's world became the responsibility of Sir Ferdinando Gorges. David's education was established to provide navigational and building trade skills. Some of the expeditions were vigorous. The world passed in front of David, where he lived, worked and loved. David built the first trading post at Odiorne Point in 1622. He brought his wife and son there in 1623.

David's thirteenth living descendent has given me permission to use the material in *First Yankee*. History cannot be altered. The purpose of this book is to introduce the school children and citizens of New Hampshire to our important founder.

The ownership of this book belongs to the Seacoast Science Center Inc., who alone has the right to print and distribute it.

David Thomson: First Yankee

London 1592-1603

David Thomson was a well-respected young man who had a thirst for knowledge in navigation and building trades. His goal was to live free in the New World and provide for his wife and family by merchant trading, fishing and furs.

At his birth, London's population was nearing 200,000. Queen Elizabeth was in the last ten years of her reign. There was a flood tide of Elizabethan Renaissance. The Elizabethan class structure was quite rigid, but some of the common folk were emerging influential, sometimes referred to as merchants of professional class. The Thomson's were members.

London's Municipal Administration was in the hands of the Guilds, which would be members of the modern day labor unions. Guild members elected city government men and the mayor. Elected city council men voted for members of its House of Commons. The Elizabethan Guild Hall would be the modern day city hall. In sixteenth century London, there were twelve guilds. The Apothecary Guild was one of them. This would become David's first trade.

David's father, Richard Thomson II, was originally from Scotland. He moved to London when young. He married Florence Cromlan on June 25, 1579 at St. James Parish in Clerkenwell, a fashionable suburb of London. He became a servant to an Army man, Sir Ferdinando Gorges. A servant in 16th Century England was not mean or menial. A servant was one who served his employer in any capacity with or without remuneration.

Sir Ferdinando Gorges enlisted in the army in 1566 at the age of 19 and earned the rank of Captain at the age of 22. He was

David Thomson: First Yankee

knighted while in France at the Siege of Rouen in 1591. He was widowed several times. Each lady brought land and money to the marriage, increasing Gorges' wealth.

Sir Ferdinando was brought to the Queen's attention by his former Commander Robert Devereux, Second Earl of Essex. Sir Fernando was appointed by the Queen to be the Governor (Captain) of the Fort at Plymouth Harbor, England's busiest sea port.

Epidemics were part of life in sixteenth century London. For a few years, the death rate would hover around three of four percent per year, then it would surge up to well over ten percent. David was born during a mild plague when the death rate was eight percent. The next year, when David's grandfather died, the death rate hit eleven percent. Ten years later, an epidemic struck Clerkenwell, taking 25% of the population, including David's father. David's oldest brother, infant Richard Thomson III died in 1582 when the Clerkenwell death rate was twice that of the preceding and succeeding years.

When a great plague struck London, there was an exodus of nobility and others who could afford it. In 1603, the King's men, an acting group with which William Shakespeare was affiliated, left London to play for several months in other towns. Physicians, who were mostly aristocrats, would usually depart the city during epidemics, leaving the task of health care of the people in the hands of the apothecaries who were the practical medical men of the time. (David Thomson later became an apothecary.)

Essex Revolt

The routines in the Gorges and Thomson households changed when Sir Ferdinando unexpectedly arrived at his Clerkenwell home from his post in Plymouth around the first of February, 1601. Gorges had been summoned by his friend and former comrade-in-arms, Robert Devereux, the second Earl of Essex, to come to London to attend a meeting set for February 3, 1601. Sir Ferdinando left his post in Plymouth without the permission of the Queen and took himself to the meeting. The London meeting was Sir Ferdinando's first step to becoming involved in the Essex treason, which resulted in the Earl's execution a few weeks later, and nearly cost the knight his life. Sir Ferdinando's folly was compounded by his being absent without leave from his Plymouth post.

The Earl of Essex was in disfavor during the entire year of 1600. His followers were frantic because they had lost all their influence at his Court. The Earl laid his troubles to Court rivals and thought that if he could only see the Queen again, he could induce her to look on him with favor.

Essex and some of his adherents began to plot how to reach the Queen. They concluded that the best means was a combined uprising of the people and an attack on the Tower by the Essex faction.

Sir Ferdinando in Plymouth was unaware of what was brewing in London. When his friend called, he responded and walked into a cauldron of intrigue in London.

Sir Ferdinando was the personification of loyalty: to his Queen, to the Earl of Essex who was his friend and commander in the European war; to Sir Walter Raleigh, rival of Essex; to Sir Robert Cecil, Queen Elizabeth's Secretary of State; and to his country. In the situation where he found himself, it was impossible for him to be loyal to all these individuals equally and simultaneously. With little or no warning of what he was getting into, he found himself "in the middle."

At the meeting, Gorges pointed out flaws in Essex's plan

David Thomson: First Yankee

such as it was. He counseled delay and tried to get promises of peaceful effort and negotiations without threatening the Crown.

The February 2 meeting adjourned with no decisions made but the scattered and diverse human forces energized by the plotting seemed suddenly to coalesce and concentrate like a tornado which touched down on earth on February 8, 1601 and quickly spent itself. Just five days after Sir Ferdinando had arrived on the London scene from Plymouth, the ill organized Essex insurrection took place and quickly collapsed.

Although Sir Ferdinando had tried to avoid violence, he was identified with the rebels. Besides, he had left Plymouth without the Queen's permission. About 200 men were arrested, including Essex and Gorges. Trials of the leaders started immediately.

After the trial, the Earl of Essex was condemned to death. He was executed in the Tower of London on February 25, 1601. It was less than a month since Sir Ferdinando had left Plymouth.

Sir Ferdinando was among the earliest to be arrested. At first, he was held by the Lord Mayor, but by February 14 he had been transferred to Gatehouse Prison. He was kept under close confinement until April 1601, constantly under the threat of trial and possible death. His property was confiscated. His post at Plymouth was taken from him, as was the income from his company at Brielle. A heavy fine was imposed but investigation showed he was already destitute. It looked like the end of his career. He became ill in prison.

November 27, 1603 he was released from Gate House Prison on bail of 1000 pounds put up by his eldest brother Edward, in whose custody he was remanded.

Sir Ferdinando went to live at Charlton in Somersetshire, a manor house near the family seat at Wraxall which belonged to his brother, Sir Edward. He was virtually a beggar, dependent

David Thomson: First Yankee

on his relatives for the bread he ate. His only hope was for military employment under the Queen or in Foreign Service.

Gorges wrote letters to Sir Robert Cecil to intercede for him. His wife and Sir Thomas Gorges pleaded with the Secretary personally. Ultimately, the Queen consented to pardon him. He at once followed up this good fortune by petitioning for the restoration of his command at Plymouth. The Queen's pardon did not include her forgiveness. Gorges could not expect to be restored to royal service as long as Queen Elizabeth lived, however, he did have his freedom and some of his property. Sir Ferdinando returned to Clerkenwell to his home and family.

Queen Elizabeth died and James I acceded to the throne in late March, 1603. The new King remembered that Essex had been one of the first to approach him secretly regarding his eventual succession to the throne. James restored to royal favor some survivors of the rebellion. Among them was Sir Ferdinando. September 15, 1603 a warrant was signed by the new King.

The two and a half years of tragedy and turmoil Sir Ferdinando and his wife, Lady Ann had endured, had been somewhat eased by the loyalty, aid and comfort rendered them by their retainers, Richard and Florence Thomson. The experience had created a bond between the families, especially between Lady Ann and Mrs. Thomson.

The death of his servant, Richard Thomson, coming just before Sir Ferdinando was ordered back to Plymouth Fort seemed to be a signal that Mrs. Thomson and David should accompany the Gorges to Plymouth.

The two older Thomson boys were already apprenticed and would remain in London with their masters. Twenty-three year old daughter, Anne Thomson, was on her own. In Plymouth, Mrs. Florence Thomson could continue to be a companion and

David Thomson: First Yankee

servant to Lady Ann. Ten-year-old David could make himself useful as a house-boy or in some other capacity.

Autumn of 1603 found the Gorges and their servants, among them Florence Thomson and her son David, residing in rural Kinterbury where Sir Ferdinando had purchased a house during his earlier tour of duty as Captain of Plymouth Fort. Kinterbury was not far from Butshead (or Budockshead) where Sir Ferdinando's cousin, Sir Tristram Gorges, had his home. The Gorges' residences were two or three miles northwest of Plymouth on the way to Saltash.

Plymouth 1603-1622

Plymouth was a major port of England for world trade: across the channel to France; to Spain and the Mediterranean; Africa, the North Sea, and the Baltic; the Canaries and Azores; Guiana and the West Indies. If one counts raiding Spanish treasure ships as part of world trade, Plymouth's trade was very profitable.

England was at peace during the years that David Thomson lived in and around Plymouth. No longer pre-occupied with war, no longer impelled or compelled to sacrifice for the common welfare, the interests of the Plymothians took new directions. Individuals, families and groups worked to promote their own ends with what means they had. Some of these ends were selfish and some altruistic. Some folks sought to serve other people, some sought to exploit them. Some people looked over the horizon to the new world and new ventures. Some looked for security nearby. The class structures were fairly rigid in England but it wasn't quite so restrictive in Plymouth. Circumstances and opportunities were favorable in Plymouth for David Thomson to become a prototype Yankee.

David Thomson: First Yankee

Plymouth Town in the early years of the seventeenth century was a walled town with narrow streets. There was little or no vehicular traffic. On land, people moved afoot or on horseback. Baggage was carried by man or beast or in a hand barrow.

About 8,000 people lived in the town of Plymouth in approximately 800 buildings compacted into an area of less than half a square mile. The houses of wealthy Plymothians could be identified by their projecting windows and stories, gable ends and barge boards and by their beautiful carved work around and about the doors and windows. Inside the houses were carved decorations, especially on staircases which had wide treads.

There were numerous 'courts' in town. These were quadrangles with houses on two or three sides. There were many inns with associated taverns where people with sea-related occupations lived when in port.

Apprentices and workmen often lived in tenements or attics at the back or atop of masters' houses. There was a workhouse or poorhouse for the native poor. Beggars, especially those from elsewhere, would be banished-beaten out of town.

The southeast end of the city defense wall was anchored by the 200-year-old castle built in the time of Henry V to guard the harbor entrance. Although gone now, its four corner towers still adorn Plymouth's coat-of-arms.

The most important building to the citizens of Plymouth was Saint Andrew's Church, located in the southwest part of the city. A new, the second, Guildhall was built in 1605 at the top of the hill north of Saint Andrew's. The hall itself was erected on arches so that the public business might be conducted above, and the butter and poultry markets carried on beneath. The sale of corn and vegetables was transacted in the adjacent streets.

David Thomson: First Yankee

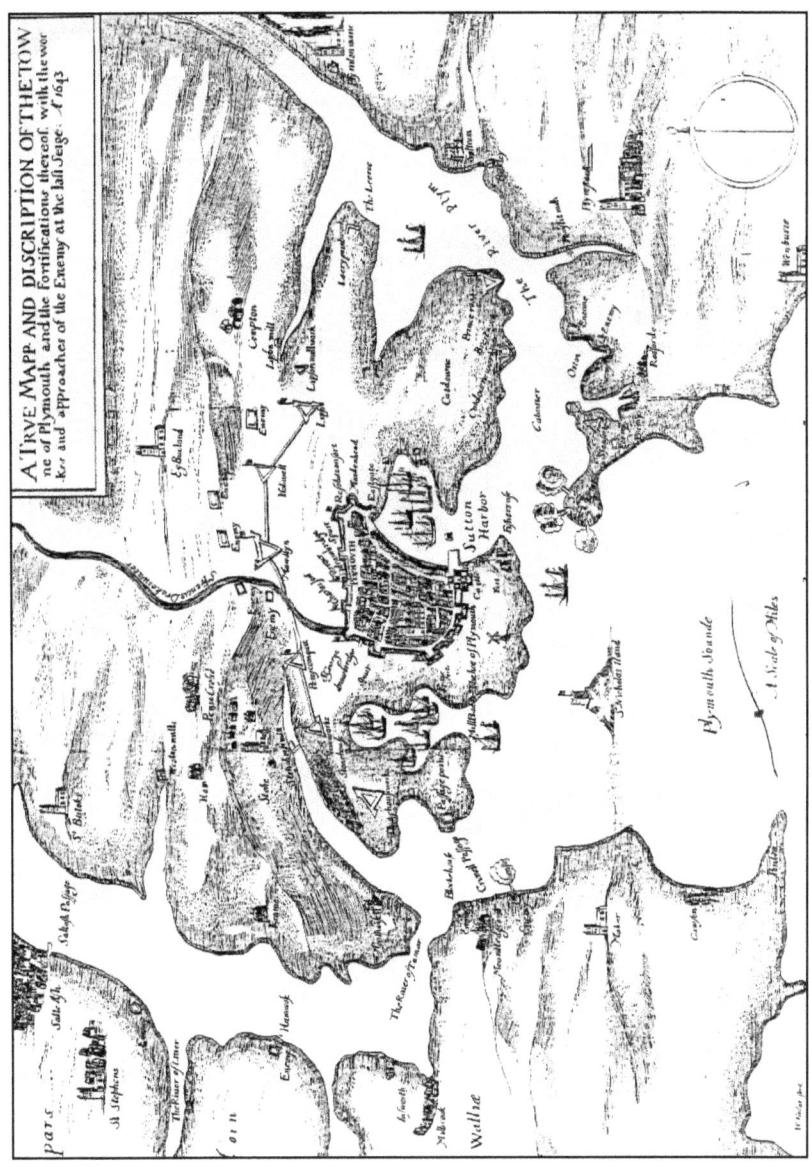

David Thomson: First Yankee

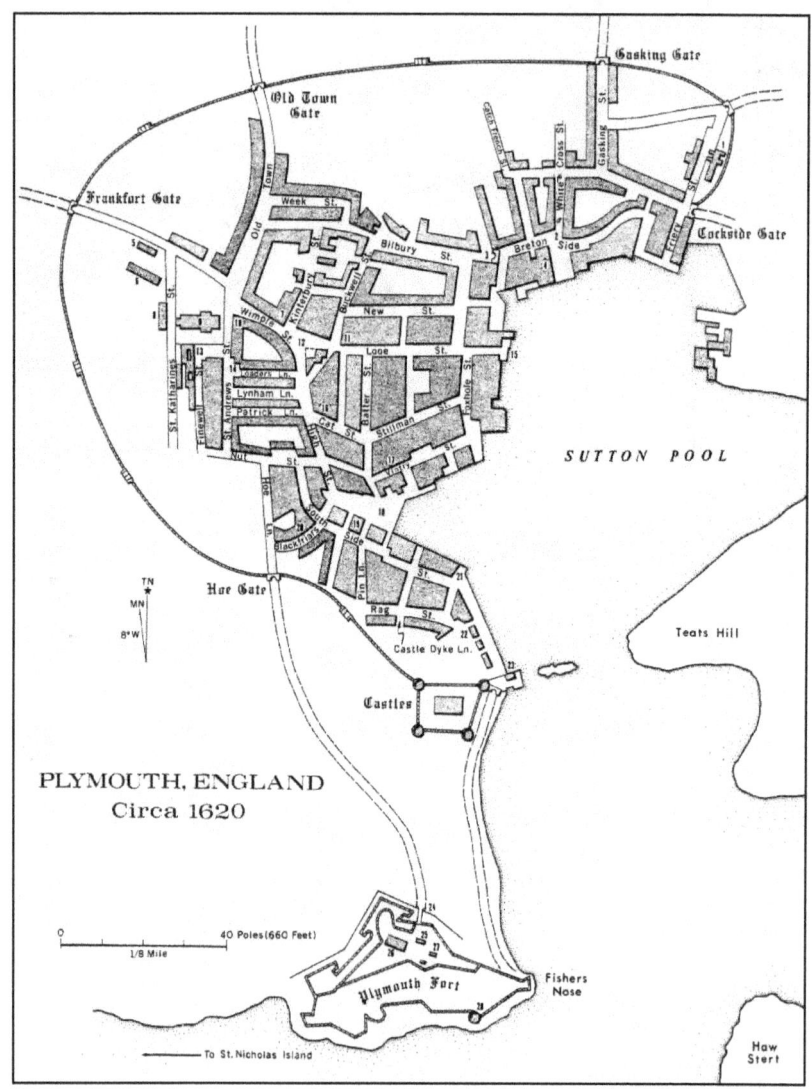

PLYMOUTH, ENGLAND
Circa 1620

David Thomson: First Yankee

The administration of affairs of Plymouth was in the hands of the Mayor and the Commonalty of the Borough. The Maisters or Burgesses of the Commonalty were chosen from among the high-ranking guildsmen of the Borough. Within the city, they had almost complete authority. The Commonalty maintained a grammar school. The Commonalty controlled all trade and commerce. Prices were fixed. Innkeepers were under strict instructions to prevent riot, and to "void" from their premises men and women of ill fame.

The Commonalty levied taxes and required licenses. They missed no opportunity of turning an honest penny by a system of fines. Generally speaking, the Mayor and the Commonalty acted for the good, as they saw it, of the town as a whole, disregarding the rights of the individual. They were not above taking advantage of their position and power to further their own interests.

The control of the city was entirely in the hands of the Commonalty, representing the common people. The nobility's power and influence over people was confined largely to the rural areas.

Employment in Plymouth was plentiful. The chief occupations were connected with the sea. Ships had long been built on the shores of Cattewater and on the east side of Sutton Pool. Shipbuilding required craftsmen and tradesmen in board, iron, pitch, tar, hemp and canvas. Fishing required sailors, fishermen and fishmongers. Not only were local fish brought into Plymouth, but large catches came from Newfoundland. Fish was Plymouth's principal export. Wine was extensively imported.

The city had to be self-supporting as far as necessities were concerned. Hence tanning, milling, building, and smiths' work occupied many. The shops and stores of the growing merchant class provided some employment.

Plymouth Fort was not under the jurisdiction of the Mayor and Commonalty of Plymouth. Plymouth Fort was the official headquarters of the Governor who was appointed by the King. The Governor of Plymouth Fort was charged with the defense of the navigable waters of Plymouth Sound. He also had charge of St. Nicholas Island which lay in the middle of Plymouth Sound and which was a key element in any defense plan.

There was a built-in conflict of interest between the 'Town and the Crown' with reference to the defense of the area. The two objectives, defense of the port and defense of the town, were not incompatible. Priorities were involved. To the Crown, the defense of the port came first; that of the town, second. Townspeople thought otherwise. The town was expected to provide the Governor with some men and funds to maintain the fort and port defenses, but the town was also expected to provide for its own defense with little or no outside help. The town petitioned the Crown, without success, to appoint an understanding Plymouth man as Commandant. The Crown feared such a man might be influenced away from his duty to the nation.

Sir Ferdinando Gorges was Governor of Plymouth Fort during this period. He was accepted by the town as well as could be expected, but tension existed. The town grudgingly met his requests, sometimes. In reality, the town supported Gorges as well as did the Crown which was quite ready to assign responsibilities to the Governor but was rather niggardly with its financial and material support. The result was that Sir Ferdinando paid much of the maintenance costs of the fort out of his own slim pockets, or from his wife's funds, and from its own commercial ventures. Perhaps this is the way the Crown planned it.

David Thomson: First Yankee

It was autumn of 1603 when the Gorgeses were established in their home at Kinterbury, 2.5 miles northwest of Plymouth. With them were Florence Thomson and her son David, and a small retinue of other servants.

At first, David made himself useful around the house and carried out such assignments as were given to him. Lady Gorges was a strong believer in education. She soon arranged for a tutor for her two sons for a few hours a day for several days a week. She and Mrs. Thomson made their contribution to the instruction. Sometimes David was privileged to participate in the lessons with the Gorges boys.

John Gorges and David, who were the same age, enjoyed each other's companionship. Robert, two years younger, resented that he was not always accepted by the older pair. He occasionally reminded David that he was a servant. However, the three boys were good friends.

It was not long before eleven-year-old David was given responsibilities of running errands between the Gorges home and the Fort or the town. He soon became acquainted with the businesses, shops, ships and personages of the town. He visited the Guildhall and enjoyed the market day activities which surged in the town square and around the base of the Guildhall.

On occasion, he carried messages to the Castle overlooking the Barbican and Sutton Pool (the inner harbor of the port.) He watched shipwrights build ships and boats on the east side of the Pool. He witnessed the loading and unloading of ships along the quay on the west side. Soldiers at the Fort demonstrated weapons of the arsenal.

On the quay, at the inns, in the shops, David met old seamen who had sailed the world from Plymouth. They told him stories of the defeat of the Spanish Armada in '88; and of sailing around the world with Drake or Cavendish in '78 and '87.

David Thomson: First Yankee

David Thomson witnessed the many fishing ships that went into and out of Plymouth waters. Some of these ships worked the nearby areas around England and Ireland. But the large catches came from Newfoundland. Some Plymouth fishermen plied the waters around Iceland and off Greenland with their hooks and nets.

There were many places around Plymouth where fish salting, drying and curing took place, especially over on the Cawsand, the peninsula at the western entrance to the Sound. The fishing industry supplied much of the food for all of England as well as the continent. Cured fish were sold up and down the coasts of France, Portugal and Spain — even in western Africa and the Mediterranean.

Thus, young Thomson at a very early age acquired a greatly enlarged view of the world. He had a rough idea of the whole Atlantic basin as well as of the Pacific and the Far East. The horizons for many of the people of Plymouth extended to the antipodes.

In the spring of 1605, Sir Ferdinando Gorges assigned twelve-year-old David to work and live at Plymouth Fort. David's duties were to help the manager of the Captain's House at the Fort. He was to be available for carrying messages from the Fort to the Gorges home in Kinterbury. He was to assist in the maintenance, repair and construction work at the Fort. He lived in the servants' quarters of the Captain's House. David could read and write. He was to be of assistance in writing messages and keeping records.

The military complement manning the Fort and St. Nicholas Island numbered about 35 men plus two or three officers. Each week a squad of men from the garrison was assigned to duty on St. Nicholas Island. They were to keep a constant vigil, noting all vessels which entered Plymouth Sound. If anything suspicious or unusual was observed, word was to be passed to the Fort.

A continuous lookout over Plymouth Sound was also maintained from the high southwest end of the Fort overlooking the harbor. When something was discovered which might need the attention of the Commander, the Officer of the Day could write down, or dictate, a message to David Thomson for delivery to Sir Ferdinando.

David would then set out from the upper fort, hike across the drawbridge over the deep ditch north of the Fort, bypass the town to the west, and make his way along paths to Kinterbury and Sir Ferdinando.

If the Officer of the Day deemed it desirable that a town official be notified of something occurring in Plymouth Sound, then David would take the message through the Hoe Gate, in the town wall, thence along Hoe Lane, turn left on Nut Street to Saint Andrews Street, turn right to Loaders Lane, right again and across High Street to the Guildhall. There the message could be delivered to the guild official.

Indians: Tahanedo, Amoret, Skicwaros, Maneddo, Sassacomoit

David became well acquainted with several kidnapped American Indians whom Gorges housed at Plymouth Fort to await transportation back to their native land.

Ferdinando Gorges learned from Captain George Weymouth that the social order of the New England Indian tribes had a class structure not unlike England's. Tahanedo was a Sagamore or chief which corresponded to English nobility. Amoret, Skicwaros and Maneddo were gentry. Sassacomoit was Maneddo's servant. Gorges recognized these distinctions when

David Thomson: First Yankee

he billeted the Indians in the Captain's House at the Fort. Tahanedo was assigned quarters nearer Gorges' official headquarters. Sassacomoit was assigned to the servants' quarters with David. Fifteen years later, Sassacomoit was known as Tasquantum or Squanto, who aided the Pilgrims at New Plymouth (Mass.).

It was conveyed to the Indians that David was to act as their guide and aide but not their servant. The Indians realized that David was a favorite of Gorges and hence was the knight's personal representative.

David's assignment was to learn to communicate with the Indians and become an interpreter. The Indians, except for Sassacomoit, were to be treated as peers of the officers of the Fort. David and Sassacomoit became particularly good friends.

Gorges did what was natural for him. As a high-ranking nobleman and born leader, he was kindly and considerate, but did not fraternize with the Indians. He had that friendly aloofness which creates respect. The Indians were proud to be the guest of this mighty commander.

David took the Indians around the Fort. They were curious about everything. He showed them the cannon and other weapons. In just a few days, the boy and the Indians were having little trouble understanding one another.

A few weeks after receiving the five Indians from Captain Weymouth, Sir Ferdinando sent Sagamore Tahanedo and Gentleman Amoret to his kinsmen near Bristol, Chief Justice Sir John Popham.

Sometimes Mr. Skicwaros, Mr. Mannedo, Sassacomoit and their guide would go into the town of Plymouth. Plymothians lived on England's doorstep to the world. They had seen people of many races, nations and languages, but American natives were a novelty. As David, with his Indians in tow, walked the

David Thomson: First Yankee

narrow streets of Plymouth Town, some people stared. Others struck up a conversation with the youthful guide.

When David was not involved with the Indians, he worked at the Fort helping with the construction or maintenance work. Occasionally, the Indians assisted. When there was a message to be delivered to Gorges at Kinterbury, sometimes one or more Indians would accompany David on his errand.

Eventually, Sir Ferdinando arranged for informal meetings with the Indians. David served as interpreter. At first, Gorges was interested in the geography. When the Indians understood what Gorges wanted, they cooperated in making rough maps showing the coastline of their part of Maine with islands, rivers, etc. They told about their customs and told their Indian names.

Association with Weymouth's Indians in Plymouth turned out to be a profound education for Gorges, for David Thomson an also for their Indian guests.

Impact of Indians

Inspired by his association with Weymouth's Indian captives, Ferdinando launched a campaign to obtain royal authority to form English settlements in the new world. He induced several leading noblemen from many parts of England to support the campaign. Within nine months after Weymouth's arrival in Plymouth, King James had granted a charter to Gorges' people giving them the right to settle two separate colonies in Virginia. The date was April 10, 1606.

The locations of the proposed settlements of the two companies were understood before the charter passed the seals. The London Company was to locate near 37 degrees North (Jamestown). The Plymouth Company was to plant near the

David Thomson: First Yankee

Sagadahoc (Kennebec) River at about 43.5 degrees North.

Sir Ferdinando Gorges and Sir John Popham elected to work with the Plymouth Company to settle northern Virginia (now New England). They agreed that each would dispatch a vessel in August of 1606 to reconnoiter the 'Maine' coast in preparation for the work of establishing the Plymouth Company's colony.

Gorges' ship, *The Richard* of Plymouth, under Captain Henry Challons, sailed from Plymouth on August 12, 1606. On board was a small company of men who were to remain in New England if it proved feasible. Also on board were two of Weymouth's Indians, homeward bound Maneddo and his servant, Sassacomoit.

Contrary to instructions, Challons took the southern route to America and was captured by a Spanish fleet near Florida. Captain, crew and passengers were imprisoned at Seville, Spain. Challons did not get back to Plymouth until 1608.

Sir John Popham's vessel, under Thomas Hanham, commander, and Martin Pring, navigator, left England in October 1606. The mission was to support the Challons expedition with additional supplies and personnel in case a settlement was started. They were also to explore. Master mariner Pring had been in New England in 1603. Sagamore Tahanedo was taken home on this voyage.

Arriving in New England and not finding Captain Challons with whom they were to rendezvous, Hanham and Pring's expedition turned to exploring and mapping. Gorges tells of the results:

"[Navigator Pring] made a perfect discovery of all those rivers and harbors he was informed of by his instructions, brings with him the most exact discover of that coast that ever came to my hands since; and

David Thomson: First Yankee

indeed he was the best able to perform it of any I met withal to this present." [1604]. *(Gorges: Narration)*

Popham, Gorges and others were so delighted with the finding, they immediately arranged for "...sending over a competent number of people to lay the ground for a hopeful plantation."

In the meantime, the London Company had also been busy. In December 1606, before Pring returned to Plymouth, the London Company's expedition to plant Jamestown left London for America.

Dr. Richard Vines

Although Gorges was impressed and pleased with the extensive and accurate geographic information brought back by Navigator Pring, he was disappointed and puzzled to learn from Commander Hanham that Captain Challons was not at the Sagadahoc rendezvous when the Hanham-Pring expedition arrived there. But Gorges received another definite bonus when the Hanham-Pring expedition put in to Plymouth in February, 1607.

Richard Vines was the 14 year old student of Martin Pring, a sea-going apothecary master on Bartholomew Gosnold's trip to Cape Cod in 1602.

Apprentice Vines and his master and other apothecaries had sailed with Captain Pring from Bristol to Cape Cod in 1603 to get sassafras, the wonder drug of the day. They had camped for several weeks at Whitson Bay, later to be known as Plymouth, Massachusetts.

Returning to Plymouth after his second trip to New

David Thomson: First Yankee

England with Martin Pring, newly certificated Dr. Richard Vines entered the employment of Sir Ferdinando Gorges in Plymouth in February, 1607. He was to serve the knight for over thirty years. Vines was to be a strong influence on David Thomson as long as the latter lived.

Plymouth Company Expedition to Kennebec, 1607

Although Sir Ferdinando Gorges and Sir John Popham were disappointed that Captain Challons had failed to get a settlement started at Sagadahoc, they determined to send another expedition under the name of the Plymouth Company to try to form a colony there. Two ships with over 100 male colonists set out from Plymouth on May 31, 1607. The larger vessel, *Mary and John*, was under Captain Raleigh Gilbert, kin of Sir Ferdinando. The *Gift of God* was captained by George Popham, nephew of Sir John Popham.

On the *Mary and John* went Skicwaros, the last of Weymouth's Indian captives to be sent home. Also on the *Mary and John*, went Dr. Richard Vines and his apprentice, David Thomson. Gorges instructed Captain Gilbert and the navigator, James Davies [1], to give his protégé, David Thomson, opportunities to learn the mariners' trade. Thomson was also to serve as interpreter in dealing with the Indians.

Before the two vessels left Plymouth, it was agreed that they would proceed independently to the Azores and rendezvous

---

[1] Navigator James Davies wrote a report of the voyage which was found in Gorges' papers in 1875. Davies: *Relation* was published in 1880 *Proceedings of the Massachusetts Historical Society*. The report was written shortly after the voyage was completed. It is liberally quoted in this story.

David Thomson: First Yankee

there at the western most island of Flowers (Flores). On June 25, the lookout on the *Mary and John* spied-

> *"The island of Gersea (Graciosa) one of the islands of the assores & it bore of us then south by east ten leagues off. Our Mr. & his mates making it to be Flowers but myself with stood them & reproved them in their error as afterward it appeared manifestly and the stood Room [sailed] for Flowers."* (Davies: Relation)

From this incident, David Thomson received a lesson in navigation. Navigator Davies explained to David that if one wished to find an island in the ocean, he should not head directly for it. Rather, he should aim for a point 10-15 leagues east or west of it. When the latitude of the destination was reached, then one should proceed west or east along the proper parallel of latitude of the island until he reaches it. If he aimed straight for the island and did not find it when he reached the proper latitude, he would not know whether to sail east or west to reach it.

Three days later the *Mary and John* entered Santa Cruse, a small town on the Isle of Flores, to take on wood and water. The *Gift of God* was there also, but there being no wind, the ships did not get together.

During the crossing of the Atlantic from the Azores to Nova Scotia, David Thomson had opportunity to learn much about ship handling, navigation, sounding, etc. Dr. Vines gave him practical instruction on coping with accidents and ailments which occurred on shipboard. David was required to memorize the names and properties of early seventeenth century pharmacopoeia.

Arriving at southern Nova Scotia, the voyagers caught great quantities of fish. While they were anchored, fishing near one of the many off-shore islands, a boat with eight-

David Thomson: First Yankee

"...Salvages & a little salvage boy...drew up to the ship...and we making signs to them that they should come aboard of us showing unto them knives, glasses, beads & throwing into their boat some biscuit but for all this they would not come aboard of us but making show to go from us we suffered them. So when they were a little from us and seeing us & three of them stayed all that night with us. The rest departed in the shallop to the shore making signs unto us that they could return unto us again the next day.

"The next day the same Salvages with three Salvage women being the first day of August returned unto us bringing wth them some few skins of beaver in another biske [Biscayan] shallop and prophering their skins to trook [trade] with us but they demanded over much for them and we seemed to make light of them so then the other three which had stayed with us all night went into the shallop & So they departed yet seemeth that the French hath trade with them for they use many French words. (Davies: Relation)

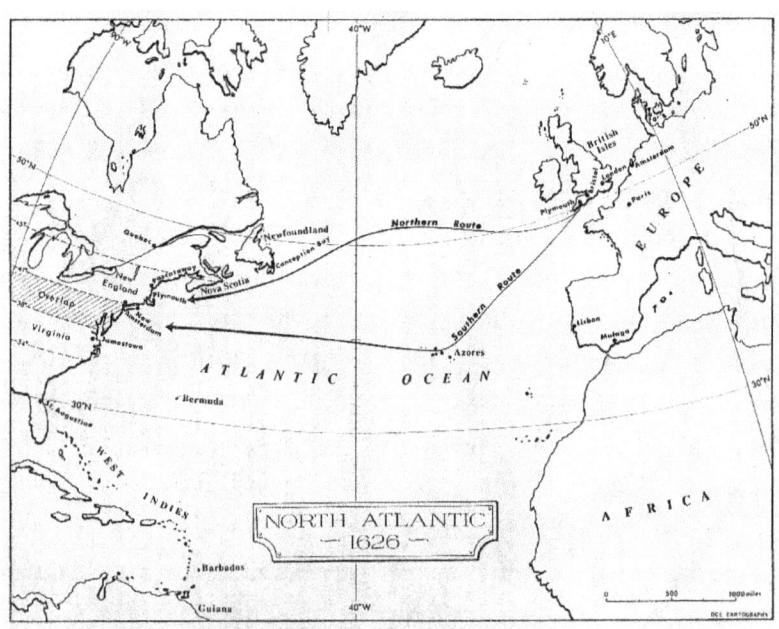

David Thomson: First Yankee

David and Skicwaros had difficulty communicating with the Nova Scotia Indians. Their language was quite unlike Skicwaros' dialect with which David was familiar. Communication was largely by gestures and signs.

Tuesday, August 4, 1607, the *Mary and John* sailed around the southern tip of Nova Scotia and turned into the Bay of Fundy, meeting with strong tidal currents. They found many islands and large fish. Realizing that they were in a great bay and that they had to go father west and south to reach their destination, which was at about 44 degrees latitude, Captain Gilbert set course west and south. Aided by favorable winds, soon they were approaching land on the northwest side of the Bay of Fundy. Then they sailed southwest parallel to the shore.

Before long, Skicwaros began to get excited. In the distance he was seeing mountains and hills that were familiar to him. Skicwaros, aided by interpreter David Thomson, began guiding the pilot, James Davies, to their destination, St. Georges Island, where in 1605 Captain George Weymouth had constructed a cross.

"Friday being the 7th of August we weighed our anchor whereby to bring our ship in more better safety how so ever the wind should happen to blow and about ten of the clock in the morning as we were standing of a little from the island we descried a sail standing in towards this island & we presently made toward her & found it to be The Gift of God. *So being all Joyful of our happy meeting we both stood in again for the island we ride under before & there anchored both together. (Davies:* Relation*)*

The 100-man expedition to plant a settlement on northern Virginia had reached its destination without loss or serious mishap. Now it became necessary to decide upon the site for settlement.

David Thomson: First Yankee

The day after the rendezvous of the two ships, Captain Gilbert manned his ship's boat with fourteen persons including himself, navigator Davies, the Indian Skicwaros, apothecary Richard Vines and his apprentice. The party rowed west to try to find the River Pemaquid[2], and hopefully the Indian sagamore, Tahanada, who after living in England for a year, had been returned to his native country by Hanham and Pring in 1606.

The Pemaquid River was only a few leagues west of Saint Georges Island. Rowing nine miles to New Harbor, the party landed. Under the guidance of Skicwaros, the pioneers hiked three miles across the peninsula to the Pemaquid.

"So the Indian Skicwaros brought us to the Salvages houses where they did inhabit although much against his will for that he told us that they were all removed & gone from the place they were want to inhabit. But we answered him again that we would not return back until such time as we had spoken with some of them. At length, he brought us where they did inhabit where we found near a hundredth of them men women and children. And the Chief Commander of them is Nahanada [Tahanada]. At first sight of them upon a howling or cry that they made they all presently issued forth towards us wth their bows and arrows & we presently made a stand & suffered them to come near unto us. Then our Indian Skicwaros spoke unto them in their language showing them what we were with when Nahanada their Commander perceived what we were he caused them all to lay aside their bows & arrows and came unto us and embraced us & we did the like to them again. Then we took our leave of them & returned wth our Indian Skicwaros with us towards our ships the 8th Day of August being Saturday in the afternoon." (Davies: Relation)

Vines and Thomson were instrumental in establishing this

---

[2] The Pemaquid was a tidal river flowing from Damariscotta Lake.

friendly contact with Tahanada and his band. David had been associated with Tahanada when the captive sagamore had first been taken to England by Captain George Weymouth in 1605. Richard Vines had sailed with Hanham and Pring when Tahanada was taken back to Maine in 1606. When Tahanada heard his English friends calling to him and identifying themselves, he had his warriors put down their bows and arrows. Friendship reigned.

"Sunday being the 9th of August in the morning the most part of our whole company of both ships landed on this island the which we call Saint Georges Island where the cross standeth and there we heard a sermon delivered unto us by our preacher giving God thanks for our happy meeting & safe arrival into the country & So returned aboard again." (Davies: Relation)

On the morning of Monday, August 10, Captain Popham took thirty men in his shallop and Captain Gilbert took twenty men, including Skicwaros in his ship's boat. They sailed and rowed to the mouth of the River Pemaquid, then up the river to the village of Tahanada's Indian band. As soon as the Indians saw the two boats loaded with Englishmen they ran to the beach with bows and arrows in hand, ready to repel invaders. Skicwaros told the Indians that the white men did not mean any harm to the natives. But Tahanada requested that the white men not land. A compromise was reached and a dozen white leaders went ashore. Finally, the Indians let all the white men land.

"So all landed we using them with all the kindness that possible we could. Nevertheless after an hour or two they all suddenly withdrew themselves from us into the woods & left us. We perceiving this presently embarked ourselves all except Skicwaros who was not

desirous to return with us. We seeing this would in no sort proffer any violence unto him by drawing he per force suffered him to remain,-and stay behind us, he promising to return unto us the next day following but he held not to his promise. So we embarked ourselves and went unto the other side of the river & there remained upon the shore the night following-Tuesday being the 11th of August we returned and cam to our ships where they still remained at anchor under the Island we call St. George." (Davies: Relation)

Wednesday, August 12, 1607, the entire expedition set sail in both ships to investigate the shores of the Sagadahoc (Kennebec) River for a site for permanent settlement. They had trouble finding the mouth of the river. They were caught in a storm and were exposed to many a hazard but by Sunday evening the two ships were safely anchored side by side inside the mouth of the river.

"Monday being the 17th August Capt. Popham in his shallop wth 30 others & Capt. Gilbert in his ships but accompanied with 18 other persons departed early in the morning from their ships & sailed up the River of Sagadahoc for to view the River & also to See where they might find the most convenient place for their plantation myself being with Capt. Gilbert. So we sailed up into this river very broad & of a good depth. We never had less water than 3 fathom when we had least, & abundance of great fish leaping above the water on each side of us as we sailed. So the night approaching after a while we had refreshed ourselves upon the shore about 9 of the clock we set backward to return & came aboard our ships the next day following about 2 of the clock in the afternoon. We find this river to be very pleasant with many goodly islands in it & to be both large and deep water having many branches in it..."

David Thomson: First Yankee

"*Tuesday being the 18th after our return we all went to the shore & there made choice of a place for our plantation which is at the very mouth or entry of the River Sagadahoc on the West side of the river being almost an Island of a good bigness, whilst we were upon the shore there came in three canoes by us but they would not come near us but rowed up the river & so past away.*"

"*Wednesday being the 19th August we all went to the shore where we made choose for our plantation and there we heard a Sermon delivered unto us by our preacher and after the sermon our patent was red with the orders & law therein prescribed & the we returned aboard our ships again-*

"*Thursday being the 20th of August all our companies landed & there began to fortify. Our president Capt. Popham set the first spot of ground unto it and after him all the rest followed & labored hard in the trenches about it.*" (Davies: Relation)

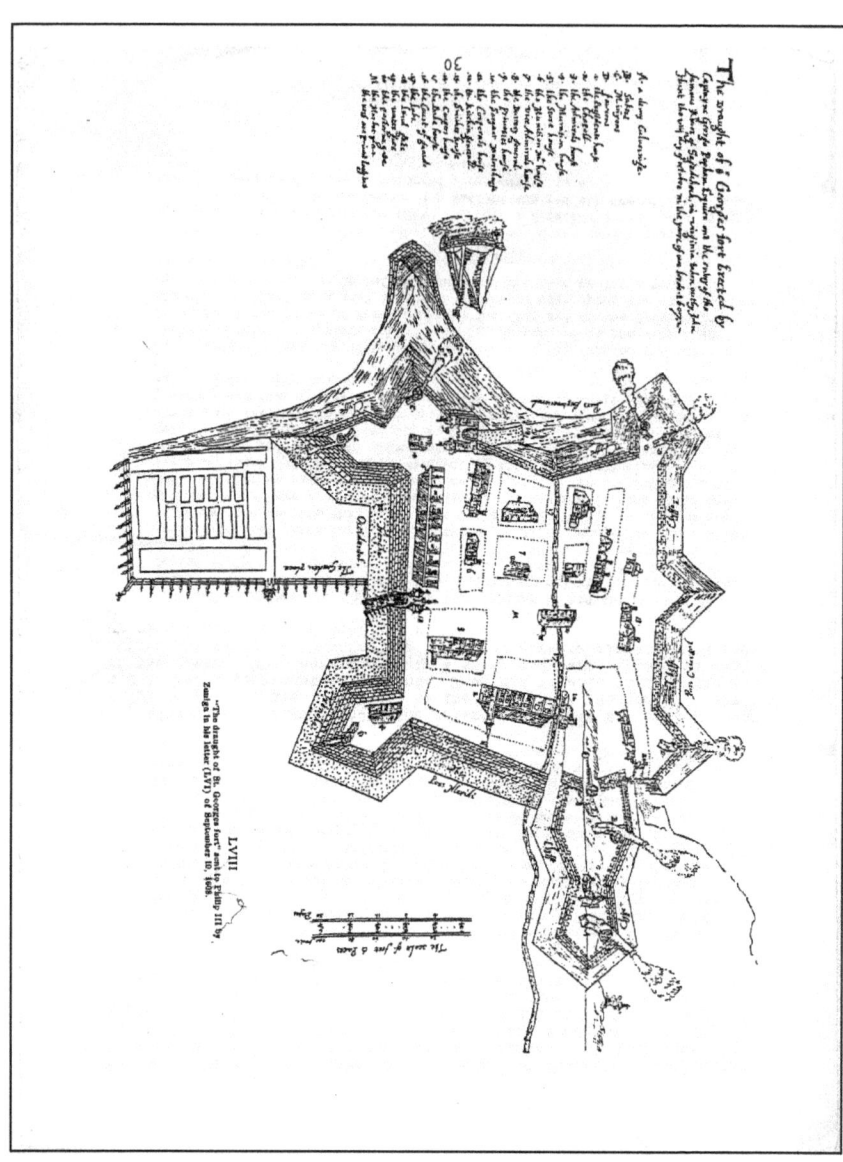

Draught of Fort Saint Georges

David Thomson: First Yankee

History of Fort Saint Georges

The "Draught of St. Georges Fort" is a photocopy taken from a copy of the original published in Brown: *Genesis*. The original plan was found in the Spanish archives towards the end of the nineteenth century. It had been sent from London to Philip III by Spanish Ambassador Zuniga along with his letter dated September 10, 1608.

Spain was alarmed at the two 1607 English expeditions to Virginia to establish plantations at Jamestown (Virginia) and on the Kennebec River (Maine). Zuniga urged King Philip to eliminate the settlements before it was too late. But Philip III did not have the drive of his father, Philip II, who launched the Invincible Armada.

Saint Georges Fort was constructed during the last five months of 1607 on a point of land (Popham Beach) at the mouth of the Sagadahoc (Kennebec) River on the western side. Indians called the place "Sabino" meaning "almost an island of good bigness."

"Each man did his best endeavor for the building of the fort...until it was fully finished, trenched and fortified, with twelve pieces of ordnance and fifty (fifteen?) houses built therein, besides a church and store house..."

"The carpenters framed a pretty pinnace of about thirty ton, which they called The Virginia.*" (Davies*: Relations*)*

The pinnace is shown in the picture on the north side of the fort.

Due to a series of unfortunate events, the Popham Colony at Sagadahoc lasted only one year:

1. Captain George Popham, president of the

colony, died of 'infirmities of age.' He was in his sixties.
2. Captain Gilbert succeeded Popham to the presidency. Gilbert's older brother died in England leaving him heir to the family estates. He had to return to England.
3. Sir John Popham, chief financial supporter of the expedition, died in England.
4. The 1607-08 winter was extremely cold. The colonists concluded that Maine was not habitable in winter.
5. The store house and most of the colonists' provisions at Fort. St. Georges burned during the winter.

Enough was enough. They all came home.

Amias

When Sir Ferdinando Gorges was re-instated as Governor of Plymouth Fort in the fall of 1603, the fort was far from being completed. For decades, new construction as well as maintenance work on the walls, barricades, ditches, roads and buildings was carried out as meager funds were available.

Plymouth shipwright, William Cole, was frequently employed by Sir Ferdinando to supply materials for, or to perform or supervise carpentry work at the fort. David Thomson was often assigned by Dr. Vines or Sir Ferdinando to work with Mr. Cole. It was through this association with shipwright Cole that Thomson acquired some of the skills which he was to use later in constructing buildings in New England.

When David was seventeen, he was directed to work with

David Thomson: First Yankee

shipwright Cole to make some minor alterations in a ship, the *Guard Star*. Cole had his 'shipyard' at the north end of Sutton Pool. The little job in the hold was progressing satisfactorily enough, when bouncing down the ladder, came a skinny, vivacious, inquisitive, not unattractive, female bundle of energy.

Mr. Cole spoke, "Ems, you know you are not supposed to come down here when we are working."

"I know, daddy, but I was bored at home and I wanted to see what you were doing." Turning to David, the girl continued with statements rather than queries, "You are Davey Thomson, aren't you."

"Yes."

"You live over at the fort."

"Yes."

"I wish I could go to sea like you do."

"Well perhaps you will someday."

Mr. Cole broke in sharply, "Ems, you go home immediately."

"Okay, daddy. Goodbye, David." Amias Cole scrambled up the ladder, ran across the deck, vaulted to the pier and skipped along the quay towards her home. Her mission accomplished.

Thus was the first conversation between David Thomson and his future wife, Amias Cole. David had known for some time that Amias was Cole's little daughter. He noted that she wasn't so little anymore. The two men returned to their work.

When the chance meeting of Amias Cole and David Thomson occurred in the hold of the *Guard Star*, Amias was within a few weeks of her thirteenth birthday. She had a carefree childhood with her earnest and somewhat dour father and her conscientious stepmother. Amias went to the Guild School and also had tutors. She had access to books and was comparatively well educated considering her sex and era.

Amias quickly blossomed into a winsome young woman, the belle of her generation, the concern of the older generation, and the darling of the oldest generation. She was blithely unconventional, venturesome but not reckless, fearless but not foolish. She was considerate, courteous, and respectful to all. She was deferent or obsequious to none. She was insensitive to class, economic, race, religious and age distinctions between people. People were people.

Children loved her; young people were a little awed by her; middle-aged folks were uneasy about her independence; but the Maisters admired her brains and her beauty.

Amias appeared to be light-hearted, even frivolous. But underneath, Miss Cole was a cool, calculating woman with objectives and priorities, and a sense of her capabilities and limitations. She possessed an intuitive feeling for strategy on how to achieve her ends.

David Thomson was an earnest, able, ambitious young man whose primary aim was to build a business in the new world and become wealthy and free. Thomson knew that long, careful preparation was necessary. He also knew that if he played his cards right, he could probably accomplish his goals.

Marriage-1613

During the years 1610 through 1612, David and Amias frequently met and spoke to each other. It was sometimes at the market on the square near the Guildhall, and sometimes on the Barbican or quay or on the street. David occasionally had assignments to work with or for shipwright William Cole when Amias might appear on the scene.

Although there was no courting as such, slowly and subtly

David Thomson: First Yankee

there grew in the minds of the boy and the girl the feeling that they were reserved for each other. The relationship was neither discussed nor acknowledged by the principals, but it was tacitly accepted by the townspeople who knew the pair.

David was a busy man with his apprentice training under Vines; with his time at sea where he took on increasing responsibilities; with his jobs for Gorges and Plymouth merchants; and in his work with Cole. He slowly accumulated a little capital.

One evening in early 1613, David was talking to Amias about his future plans. He said matter of factly, "In another year, I will have served my seven years apprenticeship with Dr. Vines. When it is completed, I think we ought to get married."

"I would like that," was Amias' poised response.

They decided not to wait. On July 18, 1613, David Thomson, apprentice apothecary, and Amias Cole, daughter of William Cole, shipwright, were united in marriage at St. Andrew's Church, Plymouth, Devonshire. Amias was not yet sixteen. David was twenty.

After the wedding Cole, David left his lodgings at Plymouth Fort where he had lived for eight years. Amias' father and stepmother made available to the newlyweds living quarters in their home on White Cross Street just below Great Tree.

Dr. Vines certified to the Governor of Plymouth Fort (Gorges) that apprentice David Thomson had satisfactorily completed his apothecary training and was qualified to practice his profession. Sir Ferdinando notified the bishop. Thus, by the end of 1613 when David turned twenty-one, he had a wife, a home and a profession. His only obligation to Sir Ferdinando and Dr. Vines were those based on friendship and loyalty, not contracts.

David now turned his attention to providing for his wife.

He served Gorges. He worked with his father-in-law on construction and alterations of buildings and boats. As occasion arose, he pursued his practice of physic.

It was February, 1615 when Amias realized she was pregnant. She told David and her parents. All were elated. April 1, 1615 Amias' father drew up a marriage settlement giving the young couple an apartment which Cole had built years before, adjoining his own home. At the ground level was a kitchen and a shop. There was a garden area behind the house which abutted the Cole courtyard next door. The first story above ground level of the apartment was a large hall. Above the hall were two chambers. A steep circular stairway built around a pole or truncated ship's mast provided access to the upper levels.

House of David Thompson

The home of David and Amias Thomson was "…neare the ould conduit in the burrough of Plymouth." The house was one of two which shipwright William Cole had built in 1595. In a marriage settlement, Mr. Cole gave the house to David and Amias who were to pay the ground rent.

In this house four Thomson children were born. Here, Amias entertained the Indian princess Pocahontas.

David Thomson: First Yankee

Harlow-Hobson Expedition, 1611

Edward Harlow, Master of Ordnance of the Sagadahoc Colony, and Nicholas Hobson, were sent by Gorges' friend, The Earl of Southampton, to America in 1611 to emphasize Sir Francis Popham's claim to the Sagadahoc. They were instructed to try to find an island supposedly near Cape Cod rumored to have gold. They were to take some 'salvages' to Sir Ferdinando Gorges for informational purposes.

The expedition visited Monhegan and Matinicus Islands and nearby Sagadahoc. They came into collision with a Frenchman named Plastrier. In the Cape Cod Area, they failed to find the island they were looking for. Their charts contained many errors which they corrected.

Harlow and Hobson had several skirmishes with the natives around Cape Cod. The expedition returned to England with five 'salvages,' one of whom was Epenow who eventually came into the hands of Gorges at Plymouth.

Captain John Smith's Map

Captain John Smith's remarkably accurate Map of New England was first published in London in 1616 in conjunction with his "book," *A Description of New England*. Hundreds of copies of the map and the book were printed. Interest in New England was greatly enhanced by their publication. Pilgrim leaders on the *Mayflower* had copies of both.

Two of David Thomson's Indian friends aided Smith in gathering data for his publications in the summer of 1614. Tasquantum (Squanto, whom Smith called Tantum) had been released from prison in Seville, Spain in 1607 or 1608 and had

David Thomson: First Yankee

made his way to London. Tasquantum was living with John Slanie, London merchant, when Captain Smith met him. Smith agreed to take Squanto back to his New England home on a fishing voyage from London. Arriving in Maine in April, 1614, they sought out Sagamore Tahanado (Smith called him Dohoday), another of Weymouth's five Indian captives who had lived at Plymouth Fort with David Thomson in 1605-1606.

While most of the sailors on Smith's two fishing ships fished in Maine waters, Smith took eight men in a small boat and ranged the coast to Cape Cod. "I have drawn a map from point to point...as I passed close aboard the shore," Smith said in his *Description*.

Dohoday and Tantum were invaluable to Smith in acting as interpreters, giving information about New England, and in correcting the charts which Smith had with him and which had been drafted by previous explorers and map makers.

Smith used Indian place names in writing his book. However, before the map was published, Smith showed it to Prince Charles. He asked the prince to choose English names for places on the map. Few of the new names stuck. Plimouth was one that did.

David Thomson: First Yankee

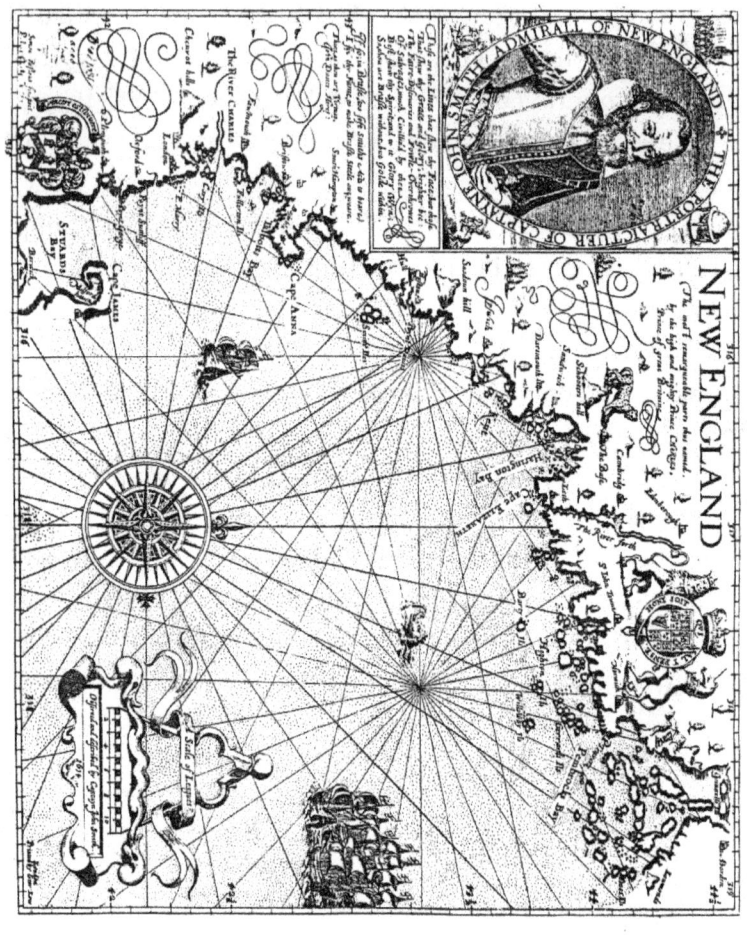

Credit: The John Carter Brown Library, Brown University

David Thomson: First Yankee

1615 Gorges sends Sir Richard Hawkins to New England

Sir Richard Hawkins, scion of the famous shipbuilding and exploring family of Plymouth[3], was president of the Second Virginia (Plymouth) Company for 1615. Gorges and his associates in the company prevailed upon Sir Richard to go to New England to find the commodities thereof and to look for intruders. Sir Richard departed Plymouth on October 15, 1615, and spent the winter in Maine. On April 20, 1616, he encountered the *Nachen*, whose commander, Edward Braunde, had sailed from Dartmouth seven weeks before. The *Nachen*'s boats were fishing around Monhegan. Hawkins seized the boats, probably regarding Braunde as a trespasser. Then Hawkins voyaged along the coast of New England.

Gorges sends Sir Richard Hawkins to New England

Gorges was discouraged. His efforts to promote settlement of New England had come to naught. His aristocratic colleagues of the Plymouth Company had lost interest, if they ever had any. They seemed convinced that it was impossible to live in frigid New England in winter. But Gorges knew better. He had had too much experience in the world to be overly concerned about blizzards. He knew there were populated countries farther north than New England which had more rigorous climates and less resources. If he could just get something started, colonizing would carry itself. Capital was needed and Gorges did not have it. Adventurers demanded large and immediate returns on

---

[3] Shipwright William Cole, David Thomson's father-in-law, learned his trade under the Hawkinses.

investments. Men were needed who were ready to work, dare and endure. Where to find them? Gorges decided he should demonstrate to the nation that Maine was livable through the winter by sending over a party of men who would spend the winter there and come back in good condition.

Gorges turned to his servant, Dr. Richard Vines. Would Vines be willing to go with a few men over to Monhegan Island on a fishing vessel in the winter of 1616? Upon his arrival there, put together a shallop, and explore the coast down to Cape Cod, searching especially for the mouths of large rivers that reached farthest into the interior where the French had discovered some great lakes? Then, in the fall, find some place on the mainland not too far from Monhegan and there spend the winter to prove that it was feasible?

In the summer of 1617, Vines and his men could return to Plymouth on a fishing vessel. For compensation, Vines and his crew would share in the proceeds from the fishing of the two seasons, 1616 and 1617. They could also keep any returns resulting from trading with the Indians.

Vines told Gorges he would go if David Thomson would be on the team. Thomson requested that in addition to his receiving shares in the two seasons' fishing proceeds, that four shillings per month should be paid to his wife in Plymouth during the time he was away. Agreement was reached between Gorges and Vines. While Vines recruited four young men in addition to Thomson for the expedition, Gorges approached his Plymouth merchant friend, Abraham Jennings, with a proposition for Gorges to share in the costs, risks, and profits of the 1616 and 1617 spring fishing season in northern Virginia of Jennings' 200 ton vessel *Abraham*. In return, Gorges was to have the privilege of sending over on the *Abraham* as passengers a half dozen men to explore and to spend the winter in America. The expedition

David Thomson: First Yankee

would return to Plymouth on a Jennings ship at the end of the 1617 spring fishing season. Gorges and Jennings reached an agreement.

Captain John Smith in *New England Trials*, speaking of 1616 says:

> "From Plimouth went 4 ships, only to fish and trade, some in February some in March, one of 200 Tons got thither in a month, and went full fraught for Spain, the rest returned to Plimouth well fraught, and their men well, within five months, odd days."

David's Dream

Undoubtedly, there was much speculation among the members of the Vines party who spent the winter of 1616-1617 at Saco. There existed opportunities for success in the new world available to men of all classes and social standing, and David Thompson dreamt of a future there. Though there are no existing records of David's thoughts at that time, it is assumed, based on outcomes, that he must have formed a detailed business plan.

He had an idea of what kind of business he wanted to set up and roughly where. He believed that Europeans could survive the winter in Maine, and even prosper. With a good English house, even women and children would be able to last the winter. There was an abundance of game and fish. He wished they had bought more corn from the Indians, but that could be remedied. He wanted to make at least one more trip to Maine to earn enough money to finance his business and to double check locations.

In addition to money from the expeditions, he had jobs lined up back in Plymouth that would add to his savings.

His aim was to build a business based on fishing but also dealing in timber, pitch, tar, furs and perhaps pharmaceuticals like sassafras and sarsaparilla roots. His market would be England and the continent.

Fishing would be an important and dependable money crop. He wanted to take better advantage of fishing than what was currently being done. Year after year, fishing ships had departed Plymouth in the early winter, sailing to Monhegan, arriving in March, catching and processing fish for six to ten weeks in the spring, and then returning to England or the continent and disposing of their cargo. There was good money in it, but there were two fishing seasons there, spring and fall. Very seldom did anyone take advantage of the fall season which ran from September through November. Thompson planned to have a year-round settlement of fishermen so that they could fish seven months of the year. The way it was then, to make a profitable single season voyage with a hundred fifty-ton ship, they must carry out 24 men to man eight fishing shallops with three men each to fish steadily for eight to ten weeks. They must also have ten or twelve men to man the fishing stages, drying racks and salting shed during and after the catching of the fish. It takes half a dozen men to stay with the ship even if it is just anchored. So, for a single fishing season, forty men are tied up for six months: two months going, three months fishing and one month returning. About a third of the men are just passengers on the ocean crossings. For two months, the ship is just waiting at anchor for its load.

A better plan was to have a gang of fishermen stay there year around. A fishing vessel could make two round trips from England a year. It could arrive around the first of July after the fish were caught and prepared, and pick up the spring catch and

David Thomson: First Yankee

take it to market. Then it could come again about the first of January after the end of the fall season and load the fall catch and take it to market. A ship would have plenty of time to take the fish to market in England and the continent of the Mediterranean or Africa, and still have a month at home twice per year – April and October. It would use ships and men more efficiently.

It was not a new idea. It had been talked about in Plymouth from time to time. When Captain Smith came back from his map-making expeditions, he advocated the idea of having year-round settlements to handle two-season fishing. It hadn't been tried because people were convinced that it was impossible to live there during the winter. However, Thompson believed year-round settlements were only a matter of time, and he wanted to be the first.

Smith's Isles (Isles of Shoals) was his location of choice. There was room along the shore at Smith's Isles for a lot of fishing stages. On shore there was plenty of room for drying racks, salt making ponds or pans and salting sheds. There was anchorage for several ships at the Isles, with enough shelter to make loading possible except in violent storms. There was room for storage sheds for the processed fish awaiting shipment. There was room for temporary billeting and messing of fishermen within five minutes of good fishing grounds.

The only problem was that Smith's Isles were no good for winter living. There was no wood, and no good soil for raising crops. The solution was to build a plantation on the big island at the mouth of the Pascataway River, the one where the two mouths of the river make it an island. On the east side of the island there was a good, deep, water port. There were plenty of trees for constructing permanent habitations and a trading post.

The big island and Smith's Isles were only a couple of

leagues apart. During the fishing season, when most men would be working from the Isles, it would be a simple matter to keep in touch with the big island base by having a boat make the round trip each day.

Thomson needed to get the legal right to operate a fishing business from Smith's Isles, and the right to make a permanent settlement on the big island of Pascataway. He also needed the need financial backing to get started with the fishing. He believed that Gorges could provide the legal rights, and hoped that Plymouth merchants would buy fish from him because they would know that Gorges would protect his legal rights, and therefore Thomson could be depended on to deliver the product promised, even as authority over and access to fishing in the New World became more contentious.

No one was using Smith's Isles or Pascataway yet. Gorges was eager to get a settlement started. He would also want a fort built at the mouth of the river. If Thomson built him that fort, it could give him a base for starting his own operations.

Thomson had experience from building at Gorges' fort in Plymouth. With such a fort as a base, he would have something concrete to sell the Plymouth merchants. He could have a trading post and a fishermen's permanent village nearby.

In addition to fishing, there were good pine trees around Pascataway and Little Harbor and up the river. Some of them grew straight and strong for a hundred feet. There would be a good market for them at home in Plymouth. Good timber was becoming scarce in England, and they could cut the timber and make lumber too, in the off-season from fishing. There wouldn't be too much of a problem about getting the timber home to England.

Thomson must have done a lot of thinking and talking along these lines. Financing and establishing such an operation as the Smith's Isles/Pascataway fishing enterprise would have required a lot of planning. Successful merchants, such as those who financed Thomson later for this project, were not the type to put their money into half-baked, wild schemes. The almost immediate success of the Smith's Isles/Pascataway operation bespeaks good planning.

1616 Pocahontas in Plymouth

May 31, 1616, the good ship *Treasurer* under command of Captain Samuel Argall[4] put into Plymouth port and tied up at Sutton Harbor's west pier below the Castles, where the *Mayflower* was destined to depart for New Plymouth four years later. Passengers on the *Treasurer* included Sir Thomas Dale, the Marshall of Virginia; John and Rebecca Rolfe and their year-old son, Thomas; Uttamatomakkin (Tomocomo), son-in-law- of the great chief, Powhatan; and perhaps a dozen natives of Virginia, mostly young females. The *Treasurer* had just crossed the north Atlantic from Jamestown.

As soon as convenient, Sir Thomas Dale and Captain Samuel Argall paid their respects to their friend, Sir Ferdinando Gorges, commander of Plymouth Fort, and to Robert Trelawney Sr., merchant and Mayor of the town.

All Plymouth was excited over the visit. Plymothians had seen male Indians from New England, but this was the first time the people had the opportunity to see an Indian women. The

---

[4] Captain Sir Samuel Argall was the "ferryman" of people and supplies to early Jamestown. In 1613, Virginia sent Argall to destroy the French settlements in New England. That same year, Argall captured Pocahontas and restricted her, not willingly, to Jamestown. Argall was governor of Virginia, 1617-1618.

David Thomson: First Yankee

entire party disembarked at Plymouth and were there for several days, resting after their long voyage and waiting for favorable winds to take them on to London.

The Indian leader, Tomocomo, had been assigned by Powhatan to count the number of Englishmen. He was to take a long stick; every time he saw a new face he was to carve a notch. "He quickly wearied of that task," according to Captain John Smith.

At this time David Thomson was in New England with Dr. Vines to explore and spend the winter there. Five months pregnant, Amias had remained in Plymouth with her father, step-mother and Bryant grandmother. Amias was well acquainted with the Trelawneys and joined the welcoming party for the Indian passengers. She was particularly interested in Mrs. John Rolfe and her baby. Rebecca Rolfe was the daughter of Chief Powhatan. Her Indian name was Mataoka or Pocahontas.

As soon as she could, Amias spoke to Mayor Trelawney, who was the father of her childhood friend, Robert Trelawney Jr. Amias requested that she be privileged to entertain some of the Indian visitors in her home, particularly the Rolfes. The arrangements were made.

Pocahontas spoke some English. She and Amias had much in common. They were nearly the same age. Pocahontas was older by a year at twenty. Both were newlyweds. They talked of children. Little John Rolfe was just a year old. Amias had lost her first baby shortly after its birth. Now, she was expecting her second.

Amias took Pocahontas through her recently acquired home, which had been built by her father for his bride years before. Her guests had come in at the ground level front entrance to the shop where David had a makeshift office and pharmacopoeia, tools and storage. In the back of the shop against a side wall was a large fireplace. Beyond was a kitchen and dining area. A rear door opened onto a walled courtyard shared with the Coles who lived next door. Here were herbs, vegetables and flower gardens.

Near the side wall opposite the fireplace was a steep, circular staircase built around a piece of a ship's mast. The guests were taken up it to the first story above ground level where there was a large hall with sleeping quarters at the rear. The second story had two chambers suitable for children, guests or servants.

The two young women told each other about social customs and more affecting women of their diverse cultures. They told of events in their lives.

Pocahontas asked if Amias knew of Captain John Smith who had been a dear friend of hers and her father's in the far away Virginia when she was a little girl eight years earlier.

"Oh yes." Amias replied. "He was here in Plymouth just a short time ago. He is in London now."

"You mean he lives? They told me he was dead."

"No, no. He is very much alive. You may see him when you get to London."

Pocahontas asked many questions about Smith. Was he a great man like a king? Amias had to hedge. He was a great man but he wasn't a king. Pocahontas sensed the hedging. She was disturbed.

As a child, Pocahontas had sat at the feet of her father's prisoner, Captain John Smith, and had listened to him tell wondrous stories of the fabulous white man's world. After six weeks of captivity, John Smith became the object of an Indian ceremony which was a combination of mock execution and salvation as a token of adoption into Powhatan's tribe. It was

David Thomson: First Yankee

Pocahontas, the chief's daughter, who was to act as the intercessor to stop the execution of the doughty captain. Subsequently her father, Powhatan, and Captain Smith became friends and sworn blood brothers. To Pocahontas, Captain Smith was like a god in the flesh, on par with and perhaps even superior to her glorious father who was supreme over all Indians. Pocahontas was the darling of these two great wereowances, Powhatan and Smith.

As a woman, Pocahontas had outgrown some of her naiveté, but in Plymouth it was disappointing to her to learn that the great wereowance of her childhood was small potatoes in the paleface world. This disenchantment about Captain Smith in Plymouth may have been the first sad experience of Pocahontas' tragic trip to England.

The word that the Indian Princess was in Plymouth reached the capital by overland messenger days before the *Treasurer* arrived on the Thames. Captain Smith in London wrote a letter to the Queen suggesting that arrangements be made to entertain the Indian Princess like royalty. The letter was ignored by the Queen; however, some people in London did try to treat Pocahontas in a manner befitting her station. In London, Captain Smith avoided Pocahontas for a while, but eventually they came face to face. Let Captain Smith tell it:

> "Hearing she was at Granford with divers of my friends, I went to see her. After a modest salutation, without any word she turned about and obscured her face as not seeming well contented. And in that humor, her husband and I, with divers other, we all left her for two or three hours..."

Later, Smith and the others returned to her presence. Pocahontas was silent for a time. Then she began to talk quietly of their days together in Virginia.

"...*You did promise Powhatan that what was yours should be his, and he the like to you; you called him father, being in his land a stranger. And by the same reason, so must I do you.*"

Smith remonstrated. Pocahontas was a King's daughter. He was the lowest of the low. She must not call him father in England. But Pocahontas broke in:

"*Were you not afraid to come into my father's Country? Did you not cause fear in him, and all his people but me? And fear you here I should call you father? I tell you then, I will; and you shall call me child, and so I will be forever and ever your countryman. They did tell us always that you were dead, and I did know no other till I came to Plymouth. Yet Powhatan did command Uttamomakkin to seek you, and know the truth, because your countrymen will lie much.*" (Smith: General Historie)

During the winter of 1616-1617, three of Pocahontas' companions had died in London. Pocahontas herself took sick. In March, 1617, almost a year after Pocahontas had left Virginia, the Rolfes left London to return to America. Pocahontas was ill and unhappy. As the *George*, under Admiral Samuel Argall, moved down the Thames, Pocahontas' illness became more serious. At Gravesend (the mouth of the Thames) she was taken ashore. There Pocahontas died.

In the parish church of St. George, Gravesend, it was recorded with pathetic indifference to accuracy:

"*1616 [1617] March 21 Rebecca Wrothe wyffe of Thomas [sic] Wroth gent. A Virginia Lady borne, was buried in the chauncell.*"

David Thomson: First Yankee

The ship must go on. John Rolfe and little Thomas went with it. But Thomas soon became ill. John had misgivings about continuing the voyage with a sick son. His shipmates advised him to land Thomas at Plymouth and to write to Henry Rolfe, John's brother, to go from London to Plymouth to take charge of the little boy.

The *George* was put in at Plymouth, Sir Lewis Stukely, Vice Admiral of Devon (soon to betray Sir Walter Raleigh) agreed to act as foster father to little Thomas until Uncle Henry Rolfe arrived from London.

It is quite probable that Amias Thomson saw the little boy again on this second visit to Plymouth.

Thomas Rolfe recovered. His Uncle Henry took him to London where he was raised and educated. He returned to his native land when he was twenty. He married and had progeny. There are now in America people who claim descent from Pocahontas and Powhatan.

David Thomson: First Yankee

Pocahontas by an unidentified artist. National Portrait Gallery, Smithsonian Institution, Washington, D.C.

David Thomson: First Yankee

1617-1618 Sir Walter Raleigh (1552-1618)

Sir Walter Raleigh, a West Country kinsman of Sir Ferdinando Gorges, was in disfavor with King James from the moment James acceded to the throne. Sir Walter's enemies convinced the King that the knight was forming a conspiracy against the Crown. Raleigh was committed to the Tower, 1603. There he languished for thirteen years. There he wrote his *History of the World* and other literary pieces.

Wearying of imprisonment and aware of the destitution of James, Raleigh hinted at the existence of a gold mine along the banks of the Orinoco River in far off Guiana, South America. Only Raleigh knew of its wealth and its location. He wished to get gold for the King, his country and himself. He assured the King that he would prefer not to live if he returned with less than a ton of slate gold ore. James signed the order for his release from prison.

Sir Walter went to Plymouth. There he organized a fleet of such power, and armed it with cannons of dimensions so unusual, that the concern of foreign ambassadors was excited. They journeyed to Plymouth port to inspect the ships, of which the *Destiny* by reason of its proportions and equipment, was the most conspicuous.

Raleigh and his fellow adventurers were profusely entertained by the municipality who rejoiced more in the freedom of Drake's companion-in-arms than in the promise of abundant bullion. Raleigh, himself, stayed at the home of Mayor Robert Trelawney Sr. When all was ready, Raleigh's crews were summoned from their merrymaking by the municipal drummer. Amidst a fanfare of trumpets, shouting of numberless voices, and the interchange of cannon between the Castle and fleet, "ten good ships of war, and three pinnaces extremely well manned,

David Thomson: First Yankee

munitioned and victualled," left the harbor. It was March 17, 1616/7. David Thomson and Richard Vines had not yet returned from their wintering expedition to New England. However, Amias witnessed the departure of Sir Walter Raleigh's fleet.

"On arriving at his destination [in South America], Raleigh found a force of Spanish soldiers lying in ambush; and taken by surprise, the exploiters were swept away. Sir Walter's son was felled by the butt end of a musket, and the survivors were compelled to run for the ships. Sick at heart, with fleet shattered, and men distracted by disaffection and doubts, Raleigh returned to Plymouth; and there, as the Destiny *lay in Hamoaze, his unhappy lady [Elizabeth] learnt the worst, and united in distress of her husband over the death of their son and the failure of the expectations. In the hope of exciting compassion at Court, they set out for London [overland]; but an officer of the King overtook them at Ashburton with words that were a premonition of death. 'I have orders,' said he, 'to arrest you and your ship.' In the anguish of despondency, Raleigh and his wife turned back, and Sir Walter was importuned at Cornwood [eight miles east of Plymouth] by relatives and friends alike to make good his escape. All had been prepared to make this easy – a barque lay in Cattewater ready to sail, and the coast of France would appear in sight with the break of the morning. Raleigh yielded to these appeals, and proceeding to Plymouth, he embarked, and, with a fair wind, his vessel made for the Channel. But his courage revived when the cliffs of England faded from view, and refusing to sacrifice his dignity for the sake of his head, he ordered the boat be put about and returned to the Barbican to face whatever accusations there might be in store.*

Stukely [who took care of Pocahontas' son], his own base relative who had recommended him to fly, was busily occupied in appropriating the cargo of the Destiny *to his own use when an imperative summons, 'all delays set apart to safely and speedily bring hither the person of Sir*

David Thomson: First Yankee

Walter Raleigh,' recalled him to an appreciation of his own risk." (Whitfield: Plymouth)

Sir Walter Raleigh was taken to London. He was put on trial and convicted. He was sentenced to death.

"In that hour, as the headsman stood by his side with the glistening axe, his [Sir Walter's] composure and serenity were sublime; and when the executioner paused, he met him with the remonstrance: 'Strike, man strike – why dost thou hesitate?' And thus passed the noblest embodiment of Elizabethan chivalry." (Whitfield: Plymouth)

The date was October 29, 1618.

1617 Vines and Thomson Return to Plymouth

We left the Vines expedition hibernating with plague stricken Indian friends at the south end of Biddeford Pool in the winter of 1616-1617. Now it was the end of February, and time to get to work. The shallop was reconditioned and refloated. It was loaded with furs, dried fish, sassafras and the party's gear. Saying good-bye to their demoralized, decimated Indian friends, the expedition shoved off for Monhegan, sixty miles away, a short sail in a brisk westerly wind.

The first of the English fishing ships were arriving. Among them was the 200-ton *Abraham*. Vines and company loaded onto the *Abraham* the goods they had collected in their year-long sojourn in New England. Then they joined with the Plymouth fishermen in their work. All realized that the sooner the *Abraham* was laden with fish, the sooner they could set out for home. The sooner they arrived home, the greater the profit. Best of all, the

David Thomson: First Yankee

sooner they could be with loved ones.

Everybody went to work with a will. Fishing shallops and small craft were taken out of storage and launched. Fishing stages (rafts) were 'ungrounded' and pushed to suitable places along the shore and anchored. Wooden fish-drying racks on the shore were refurbished or rebuilt. Simple eating and sleeping arrangements were put into operation. Practically all the Plymothians were experienced. They worked well as a team. The work of catching, splitting, drying and stowing fish went on apace.

By the end of May, the *Abraham* was loaded and ready to depart. Wafted by the prevailing westerlies, it made a fast voyage across the ocean. They reached home in Plymouth in early July, 1617.

David Thomson was glad to get home to his beloved Amias and to find her well. Little Prissilla was eight months old when she first saw her father. It was a happy reunion for the Cole in-laws and the Thomsons.

Amias told David about the birth and activities of the baby. She told about her pleasant associations with Mrs. Rolfe (Pocahontas), the Indian woman from Virginia, who had visited Plymouth on her way to London from Jamestown. David learned that Pocahontas had died shortly after leaving London for a return voyage to America.

Amias told David about Plymouth's send-off for Sir Walter Raleigh to go to Guiana to seek out a fabulous gold mine. David would soon be a spectator to the sad return and arrest of Raleigh at Plymouth. Later he would learn of his execution in London.

Mr. Cole reported on the progress of the construction of the 'poor house' or work house called Orphans' Aid. He complained of how difficult it was to get structural lumber of any sort in England. Fifty years earlier, it was thought that the forests of

England were inexhaustible, but now they were gone. People froze during the winter because there wasn't any fuel. The development of coal or peat for fuel was not happening very quickly.

David told of the vast timber resources in New England. He hoped that it could be made available to England.

Vines, Thomson and the young men of the expedition were the momentary heroes of Plymouth. The townspeople had just gone through a hard winter with a minimum of fuel. What impressed the citizens most was the tale told by the explorers of having unlimited firewood to burn in their cabin fireplace during the winter.

To Sir Ferdinando Gorges, the 1616-1617 Vines exploration and wintering expedition to New England was a complete success. He was elated. After many failures and frustrations, perhaps Dame Fortune was turning his way. He should have no trouble getting adventurers to go to New England now.

Gorges was very pleased with the detailed reports which Vines and Thomson made to him. During their absence, Captain John Smith's *Map and Description of New England* had been published. Gorges had copies. Between Smith's works and the oral and written reports by his servants, Gorges broadened his knowledge of New England. His enthusiasm increased. Nevertheless, 'adventurers' did not come knocking at his door.

David Thomson's ambitions for exploiting economic opportunities in New England continued to burn bright in his breast in Plymouth. His plans became clearer in his mind with the passage of time. He knew what he was going to do. He was going to become wealthy and free in America. David was determined to reach his goals of wealth and freedom for himself and his family in New England. It was not that David felt oppressed in England, but rather that in America, one felt free.

David Thomson: First Yankee

In New England one could become one's own boss. Almost as soon as he got back to Plymouth in the summer of 1617, he acquired copies of Captain John Smith's *Map of New England* and of Smith's brochure, *A Description of New England*, which had been published in London in 1616 while David and Vines were exploring the New World. What David read in Smith's *Description* did not diminish his zeal:

"...*here [in New England] every man may be master of his own labor and land; or the greatest part in a small time. If he have nothing but his hands, he may set up his trade; and by industry quickly grow rich; spending half that time well, which in England we abuse in idleness, worse or as ill.*" (*Smith:* Description)

Twenty-four year old David told his beloved twenty year old Amias of his dreams, or rather of his objectives and strategy for his life work. Detailed plans and tactics could be worked out as his promotion campaign progressed. Right now, he knew where he was heading. He would need financial support and the cooperation of wealthy merchants. He would also need the 'political' assistance of Sir Ferdinando. David was determined that those who aided him should be compensated in some way for their assistance. It must be quid pro quo. Amias was agreeable to David's aspirations.

David knew he would have to bide his time, but this would give him time to prepare himself to cope with the businesses he aimed to conduct. He would also have opportunity to cultivate those people with whom he hoped to deal for support.

Vines and Thomson had already reported to Sir Ferdinando that the only river that seemed to give promise of tapping large interior lakes was the Pascataway (Piscataqua). The Merrimac was a big river, but natives said that they did not know of a big

David Thomson: First Yankee

lake at its head. David told Gorges that he might be interested in exploiting the fur trade and timber of the Piscataqua.

Vines and David had also reported to Gorges that Massachusetts Bay seemed to be a good port for a town. David told Gorges that it was also a good place for Indian trade. It was some distance from the best fishing zones so there would be less competition from fishermen trading with natives. David said that the Bay appealed to him for its economic potential.

Amias' father, shipwright William Cole, often serviced the fishing vessels of Plymouth merchants. Amias had grown up and gone to school with the children of the men who were not in charge of the town. Having occasionally worked on ships with Cole, and having married Amias, David Thomson was acquainted with and was accepted by many wealthy guildsmen. The merchants were interested in David's New England experiences and findings during his thirteen month stay there. David had several opportunities to tell Plymouth ship-owners about the Isles of Shoals and to speak of the possibilities of fishing from them. He also mentioned that he would like to have a piece of the action.

David spoke often to his father-in-law on the unlisted quantities of timber around Pascataway. David hoped that he and Cole might be privileged to participate in the exploitation of New England forests.

By 1618, David Thomson had started his campaign toward materializing his dream.

Amias quickly became adjusted to the idea of going to America. For a long time she had sensed that it was likely to happen. She began to look forward to the great adventure.

Little Prissilla was a toddler in the summer of 1618. Amias was pregnant again. In January 1619, two-year-old Prissilla acquired a little brother, John. Less than six weeks later,

David Thomson: First Yankee

Thomson again sailed for New England, this time with Captain Thomas Dermer.

Dermer – Squanto Peace Missions in New England

During the summers of 1619 and 1620, Captain Thomas Dermer and Squanto (Tasquantum, Tantum) toured the coast of New England seeking to establish better relations between the natives and the English. They also traded and explored.

Sir Ferdinando Gorges said in his *Relation* (published in 1622) that it was Dermer's and Squanto's peace efforts of 1619 and 1620 which made possible the success of the Pilgrim settlement at New Plymouth in 1621. Pilgrim Governor Bradford, of Plymouth Plantation, disputes Gorges' claim. Branford gives all the credit to God.

Dermer sent a letter from Newfoundland to Gorges in Plymouth via a fishing vessel requesting him to send a commission and supplies to Dermer at Monhegan to permit him to undertake the proposed peace mission. Gorges immediately sent Captain Rocraft to Monhegan to intercept Dermer and Squanto, but Dermer was unable to get to Monhegan.

After waiting in vain some months in Newfoundland for transportation to New England, Dermer took Governor Masons' advice and sailed on a fishing vessel for Plymouth with Squanto.

Smith (*Trials*) Speaking of 1619 says:

"This year there went a ship of 200 tons who stayed in the country about six weeks, with 38 men and boys, and had her fraught...Mr. Thomas Dermer having lived about a year in New-Found-Land, returning to Plimoth, went for New England in this ship...He stayed there with five of six men in a little boat: finding 2 or 3 Frenchmen

David Thomson: First Yankee

among the savages, who had lost their ship; augmented his company, with whom he ranged the coast." (Smith: *Trials*)

Telling about Dermer's 1619 Goodwill expedition in New England, Gorges said that Dermer "... shape his course from Sagadahoc in forty-six degrees to Capawack, being in forty-one degrees and thirty-six minutes, Sending me a Journal of his proceeding with a description of the coast all along as he passed."

Evidently when the Dermer party left Monhegan Island on May 19, they went first to the mainland. Squanto and Thomson were familiar with this area. They visited with the Indians. Through Squanto, Dermer told sagamores that more Englishmen would be coming to New England. Dermer wanted the sagamores' council to devise policies and means by which natives and Englishmen could live and trade in peace and harmony.

At Pemaquid or Sagadahoc, the Dermer party must have met the Indian, Unnangoit. English fisherman had dubbed him Captain John Somerset. Captain Christopher Levett, writing about Somerset and 1624 (Levett: *Voyage*) described Somerset as "... a sagamore, one that hath been found very faithful to the English, and hath saved the lives of many of our nation, some from starving, others from killing." It was Somerset (the Pilgrims knew him as Samoset) whose brave, dynamic and skillful action may have saved the new Plymouth colony from annihilation by Indians. Here is what Somerset did to establish peace between the Pilgrims and the Indians

For more than four months after the *Mayflower* had made landfall at Cape Cod, the Pilgrims had been unable to make any friendly contact with their Indian neighbors. Then on Friday, March 16, 1621, Samoset (Somerset):

David Thomson: First Yankee

"... very boldly came all alone and along the houses straight for the rendezvous, where we intercepted him, Not suffering him to go in, as undoubtedly he would of his boldness. He saluted us in English and bade us 'Welcome.' For he had learned some broken English among the Englishmen that came to fish [New England waters] and knew by name the most of the captains, commanders and masters that usually came there." (Mourt's: *Relation*, 1622)

In just one week of masterful manipulation of Indians in Englishmen, Somerset had:

    1. Instituted trading between the Pilgrims and local Indians.

    2. Had tools returned which the Pilgrims had left in the fields and which had been taken by Indians.

    3. Brought Squanto from Namasket to the pilgrims and ordered him to serve them as interpreter which she did for the remainder of her life.

    4. Induced Indian King Massasoit to go to New Plymouth and have a pow-wow with the Pilgrims. This resulted in a treaty which lasted for decades.

On Friday, March 23, 1621, Somerset left New Plymouth and returned to his home in Pemaquid, Maine.

After consultation with Indian groups at Sagadahoc, Dermer and party cruised the coast southerly. When they came to Accomack (site of New Plymouth), they learned that all of Squanto's Patuxet tribesmen were dead. Accomack was deserted.

David Thomson: First Yankee

Squanto led the party overland west from Accomack fifteen miles to Namasket where they found an Indian village. From Namasket sent a messenger further west to Pocanocket (Rhode Island) to invite Pocanocket (Wampnoag) chiefs to come to Namasket for a conference. A day or two later, two Kings attended by a guard of fifty armed men, came for the meeting.

It was less than two years later (March 1621) that Samoset (Somerset) and Squanto brought the 'great Sagamore' Massasoit, Chief Sachem (King) of the Pocanockets (Wampanoags), his brother Quadequina, and sixty men to New Plymouth. In one week, a peace pact between the Indians and the Pilgrims was completed. It is probable that many of the Indians who conferred with Dermer at Namasket in June 1619 were the same as those who treated with the Pilgrims at New Plymouth in March 1621. Perhaps the groundwork for the later Pilgrim treaty was laid at Namasket in 1619.

The 1619 meeting of Dermer and the Pocanocket King (Massasoit) must have been tense at times. Dermer reported in a letter to Gorges dated June 30, 1620:

"The Pocanockets, which live to the west of Plymouth, bear an inveterate malice to the English, and are of more strength than all the savages from thence to Penobscot. Their desire for revenge was occasioned by an Englishman, who having many of them on board, made a greater slaughter with their murderers [ship's guns] and small shot when as (they say) they offered no injury on their parts. Whether they were English or no it may be doubted, yet they believe they were for the French have so possessed [convinced] them. For which cause Squanto cannot deny but they would have killed me when I was at Namasket, had he not entreated hard for me."

Dermer redeemed a French captive of the Pocanockets at Namasket; the Frenchman joined Dermer's crew.

David Thomson: First Yankee

After the parley, Dermer, Squanto, Thomson, the Frenchman and a few others hiked back the fifteen miles to New Plymouth (Accomack). They retrieved their boat and proceeded around the Cape to Capawack.

On the voyage back to Monhegan from Capawack, Dermer put in at Massachusetts Bay, where he held another Conference with Indian leaders. He redeemed another French captive of the Indians. The party also visited Thompson's Island in the Bay as is evidenced by a deposition by the Sagamore of Agawam to the Massachusetts court many years later.

David Thomson desired to re-examine Smith's Isles (Isle of Shoals) where he planned to establish a fishing base. He wished to make a chart of the little archipelago and check on its latitude. As the expedition neared the Isles from the south and was about a quarter mile from an isolated rocky islet, a boatman thought he heard shouting. The crew quieted and soon they spied an Indian boy waving his arms and signaling for help. The pinnace was turned and made for the islet. They young native was rescued.

It seems that the Indian lad a few days earlier had set out from the mainland alone in a small canoe to explore the islands which he could see from his home. Caught in a squall, he made for the nearest land which was the islet. His craft was wrecked on the rocks and he was injured. He also was stranded. The larger islands were too far for him to attempt to swim in his condition. Besides, they were uninhabited. He had resigned himself to his death when the rescuers appeared.

Sailing between and charting the principal islands of the archipelago, the expedition wended westerly to the nearest point on the mainland. It was near Pascataway. As they approached the shore, a few curious Indians gathered. When the Indian boy yelled a greeting to them, the Indians on the beach

David Thomson: First Yankee

broke into shouting.

Four and a half years later, this Indian lad, grown into a young man, was given by his Sagamore to David Thomson. He was given the English name of Watt Tylor.

The party spent the night at Pascataway. Dermer invited the Indians to bring any skins they had to trade. Generosity was shown on both sides and the trading was successful.

Two days later, the explorers rounded the cape before the mouth of the Saco River and pulled into the Biddeford Pool to camp for the night. David Thomson showed his associates the cabin where he and Captain Vines' party had spent the winter of 1616-1617 with the Indians. He told how many of the Indians had died of the plague but that none of the Englishmen became ill.

While he was talking to his countrymen, a couple of Indian braves were observed watching the white men from among the trees a few poles away. David Thomson hailed the braves. There was a reunion. Both of the Indians were well acquainted with David from three years earlier. One of the braves dashed off to notify his tribesmen of the presence of David Thomson and Squanto. Soon there were a dozen natives in the gathering. There was an exchange of gifts.

The next morning, the Dermer expedition took leave of their Indian friends to continue their journey back to the *Abraham* at Monhegan Isle. Squanto decided that since he no longer had relatives at Accomack, he would stay with his new and old friends at Sawaguatook (Saco).

From Biddeford Pool, the peacemakers sailed directly to Monhegan Island, where they arrived in the late afternoon on June 23, 1619. The crew and fishermen of the *Abraham* were ready and eager to depart for home after a successful season. Their shallops and fishing stages were stowed to await next

David Thomson: First Yankee

year. With luck, the *Abraham* could be home at Plymouth in a month.

Dermer sent a report to Gorges by Thomson who returned on the *Abraham*. Dermer and the small crew, including the two redeemed Frenchmen, sailed for Virginia. Dermer wrote Purchas from Virginia in December that he had some trouble with Indians in the absence of Squanto.

Early the next year, 1620, Dermer returned to New England from Virginia to continue his combination goodwill, exploration and trading efforts. He picked up Squanto at Saco and proceeded to Monhegan, where he met ships that had just arrived from Plymouth for the new fishing season. Dermer was given a letter from Gorges telling him that settlement in New England for this year or the next did not look promising because of opposition in Parliament to the new charter. Gorges told Dermer he could discontinue his peace efforts if he wished and return to England, but Dermer decided to carry on his work.

Dermer sent a letter to Gorges in Plymouth via a Plymouth ship. It was dated June 30, 1620. Some time after sending the letter, Dermer and Squanto turned south again. On Capawack, the little party was attacked by some 'new' savages. Dermer was severely wounded, but was able to get to Virginia where he died. Squanto returned to the mainland where he made his home at Namasket, fifteen miles west of his childhood home at Accomack. It was summer, 1620. The Pilgrims arrived at Cape Cod just a few months later.

The reader may judge what contribution to the safety and success of the Pilgrim colony at New Plymouth was made by Dermer and Squanto's peace efforts in the spring and summer seasons of 1619 and 1620.

David Thomson: First Yankee

Summer 1619, David is Home Again

The last of July 1619, the *Abraham* hove into Plymouth with its cargo of fish from the New England main. Relatives of the sailors and fishermen rejoiced to learn of the successful voyage. On board was David Thomson, returning from his explorations with Captain Thomas Dermer and delivering Squanto to his home country. Thomson had with him the soil samples which Dermer had procured from an island near Cape Cod. He had many furs. He also had Dermer's written report to deliver to Sir Ferdinando Gorges.

Debarking at the quay in Sutton Pool, David was met by his wife, Amias; his two-year-old daughter, Prissilla; and his seven-month-old son John, who had been only six weeks old when his father left Plymouth. The next day, Thomson walked to Kinterbury to give his and Dermer's reports to Sir Ferdinando. Then he walked back to take up his life in Plymouth.

Sir Ferdinando Gorges Seeks a New Charter

For fifteen years prior to 1620, Sir Ferdinando Gorges' burning desire had been to promote settlement of New England by Englishmen to the glory of God, the King and England. Gorges, never a wealthy man, had kept himself poor by devoting every penny he could lay his hands on to the furtherance of his project. His first duty had always been the defense of his country. This took some of his money and most of his time. It required him to remain at his post as Commander of Plymouth Fort. But now, 1619, international tensions were somewhat relaxed. Gorges could leave his command in charge of a new deputy and devote more of his time and attention to his dreams for a *new* England

David Thomson: First Yankee

in New England. There would be great estates and manors of noble gentlemen with their loyal yeomen and retainers. There would be cities controlled by guildsmen representing all crafts. There would be trade between old and new England. A tolerant Church of England would serve religious needs. All would be loyal to the Crown.

Reports from John Smith, Vines, Dermer, Thomson, fishermen, Indians and others had given Gorges all the information he needed about New England. Now he was ready to push harder toward colonization. He believed he need greater authority from the Crown in order to work effectively. The 1606 charter setting up the two Virginias (1. London Company, First Colony, or South Virginia; and 2. Plymouth Company, Second Company or North Virginia) had given each Virginia group permission to effect settlement in and possess a piece of territory stretching for one hundred miles along the coast and one hundred miles inland. The 1606 charter provided that the Virginias' settlements should be governed from England by a Royal Council for Virginia.

The Royal Council had never been created. Since 1606, the south Virginia Company had obtained two new charters which greatly extended its territory and which had enabled it to assume many powers of self-government. Since there had been no permanent settlement established in north Virginia (New England), any settlement formed there now would have come under the original charter (1606) which had not been implemented with respect to the government.

If north North Virginia was to be colonized, there would need to be some provision for control. If settlement was to be financed in part by fishing, as Gorges had planned, the sponsors of the colony would need jurisdiction over the sea adjoining the land.

David Thomson: First Yankee

A few months after David Thomson reported to him about Dermer's 1619 mission to New England, Sir Ferdinando Gorges left Plymouth for London to promote at Court his plans for greater authority over colonization of north Virginia. Sir Ferdinando had decided that an entirely new charter from the throne was needed. This new charter must empower a 'Council' to make land grants to prospective settlers, and to have authority to provide for a colonial government.

When rumors circulated of a new charter for north Virginia, which permitted taking of fishing in New England, there was immediate objection. It grew stronger when the formal petition for a new charter was presented to the King on March 3, 1620. The proposed charter gave a proposed governing council a monopoly over affairs in New England. The council would be empowered to grant licenses for trade and to expel intruders. Its jurisdiction would extend one hundred miles out to sea. Implicit was the power to control (tax) fishing.

The south Virginia Company (Jamestown) fought the proposed New England charter, claiming that New England fishing should be free to everyone, or at least to all Englishmen. Ratification of the charter by the King's Privy Council was stalled for many months.

1619-1620 David in Plymouth

After returning from the hastily arranged voyage with the *Abraham* to New England, David Thomson came back to his ordinary routine in Plymouth. He worked with his shipwright father-in-law in the construction and repair of ships, boats and buildings and also the increasingly difficult task of procuring from near and far scarce wood products for building material.

David Thomson: First Yankee

Construction on the Orphans' Aid building was progressing and there were occasional jobs at the fort both of which sometimes required Cole's expertise.

People from in and around Plymouth often sought out apothecary Thomson for medications, medical advice and treatment. David tried to keep his pharmacopeia stocked with local, national and foreign pharmaceuticals. David was happy to be home with his wife and two children. The parents enjoyed some social life with other enterprising young couples of the community.

In addition to his reporting to Sir Ferdinando on his last trip to New England, David had other conferences with his former patron. Thomson learned about Gorges' hopes, plans and intentions regarding settlement of New England. He was not unsympathetic to Gorges' design to have fishing support colonization.

After talking with Gorges, David felt a sense of urgency to go forward with his own personal plans for moving to New England before it was too late. He sought audience with the wealthier Plymouth merchants, whose ships or wealth were often used for fishing expeditions to Iceland, Greenland, Newfoundland and New England. These were such men as the Sherwill brothers, Thomas and Nicholas; Leonard Pomery, Abraham Colmer, Abraham Jennings, Thomas Ceely and three father and son combinations with the same names: the John Jopes, the John Clements and the Robert Trelawneys. (The Jope, Clement and Trelawney sons were young adults about the same age as David and Amias. There is evidence that the young folks were well acquainted.) Nearly all of these men served at least one term (one year) as Mayor of Plymouth.

Thomson's sales pitch to the Plymouth merchants was that he thought that commercial activity in New England was going

David Thomson: First Yankee

to increase rapidly in the near future and that he thought the Plymouth people should pre-empt the Isles of Shoals as a fishing center before others got the same idea. The Isles were right in the middle of excellent fishing banks. There were good sites on them for stages, for fish drying racks and salting sheds, and for salt making ponds. There was room for off-season storage of boats, stages, etc., and there was protected anchorage for ships.

More specifically, David Thomson's proposal to the Plymouth merchants in early 1620 was that they institute a plan advocated by Captain John Smith and others, that of having a crew of fishermen live in New England all year round so they could fish during both the spring and fall fishing seasons. The fishermen would not have to spend three months going to and from England; the sailors and their ships would not have to mark time in New England waiting for the fish to be caught and processed.

Thomson told the merchants that Sir Ferdinando Gorges planned to exploit the Piscataqua River as a highway to fur trade around the lakes thought to be in the interior. Thomson expected to assist the knight in his project. Thomson also wanted to profit from fishing as well as from fur and forest products. He would like to team up with Plymouth merchants in their New England fishing.

Thomson said that when Sir Ferdinando received his new charter, Thomson expected to get a patent for some land at the mouth of the Piscataqua River and move his family over to New England. He would set up a trading post there. If the Plymouth fishermen worked from the Isles of Shoals during the fishing seasons, they could live during the winter on the nearby mainland where the Thomsons were located. Thomson could superintend the fish catching and processing by the Plymouth fishermen at the Isles of Shoals during the spring and fall fishing

David Thomson: First Yankee

seasons for a share of the profits. He could operate his trading post and lumber business at the mouth of the Piscataqua in which enterprises the Plymouth merchants could share in the profits for handling the transportation to, and the marketing in, Europe.

David urged his merchant friends to send one or two ships to the Isles of Shoals right away to try out the fishing there and establish a claim to the site based on usage. If Plymouth fishermen were already using the Isles of Shoals as a fishing center when Gorges got his new charter, their priority would be recognized.

Although in some of their commercial enterprises the Plymouth merchants were competitors, in their New England fishing activities they usually cooperated. They saw merit in Thomson's scheme to get control of the Isles of Shoals for a fishing center. Plymouth merchants sent an expedition from Plymouth to the Isles of Shoals in early 1620. The mission was to start using the Isles for a fishing base for Plymouth ships. The expedition was a success.

Summer 1620, The *Mayflower* in Plymouth, Devon

Early Saturday morning, August 26, 1620, two ships, strangers to observers on the Hoe, came sailing into Plymouth Sound and past Saint Nicholas Island. They flew white ensigns bearing the red cross off rounded Fisher's Nose and under the fort and drew up toward the quay near the Barbican. Curious townspeople came out of the narrow streets. They stared at the ships carrying men, women and children bound for the new world. The passengers in their crumpled clothes and dirty, nervous faces crowded the sides of the ship and gazed longingly at the town.

Here was ordered living; neat houses three or four stories tall, and all the comforts of civilization they were soon to leave forever.

The two masters, Christopher Jones of the *Mayflower*, and Captain Reynolds of the *Speedwell*; two governors, Christopher Martin of the *Mayflower* and Deacon Robert Cushman of the *Speedwell*; and Deacon John Carver and Elder William Brewster, sought consultation with the Mayor and Council. They were led along the quay to the end where they walked up Southside Street, then turned right on Pin Lane to cross the New Quay. Eventually, they came to the official Mayoral House on Vintry Street. Mayor Robert Rawlyn was not in, so the group walked up High Street to the Guildhall were the Mayor and a few councilmen had assembled anticipating a call from the emigrants.

The newcomers' needs were quickly stated. The smaller of their two ships, a pinnace, the *Speedwell*, was leaking and proving unseaworthy. Services of shipwrights were necessary to find the trouble and to make repairs. Their funds were low, in fact they had to sell some of their precious supplies to pay for similar services in Southampton and Dartmouth, but they would pay. In the meantime, they would like their passengers to have some freedom of the city.

William Cole and two other shipwrights agreed to inspect the *Speedwell* and try to make repairs.

There is no record of where the Pilgrims stayed in Plymouth during the Mayflower's twelve day stop there in 1620. It is likely that the Plymouth city fathers offered them the use of the shelter of the hospital of the Orphans' Aid building which had just been

David Thomson: First Yankee

Hospital of the Orphans' Aid
Plymouth England   construction 1615 to 1620

Matthew R Thompson III

completed on Saint Katharine's Street across from Saint Andrew's Church.

The principal promoters and donors for the construction of Orphans' Aid were the same Plymouth merchants and guildsmen who were the financial sponsors and partners for David Thomson's enterprises in New England.

Records show that David Thomson's father-in-law, shipwright William Cole, worked on the construction of the Orphans' Aid building. It is quite possible that David Thomson did also.

The hospital of the Orphans' Aid building served as a workhouse, dormitory and school for centuries. It was destroyed in the World War II bombing of Plymouth. Saint Andrew's Church was also damaged by the bombing, but it was repaired.

Many of the townsmen had long sympathized with the demands of Brownists for freedom of congregational worship. There was sympathy with this community of humble folk who had crossed to Holland in search of a freer atmosphere. The town had a strong Puritan element who were dissatisfied with the way the Church of England was functioning. Among these were several members of the commonalty such as the Sherwill brothers, Thomas and Nicholas. Here was an opportunity to help these brethren in their hazardous venture of conscience.

When the women passengers heard the news, some of them wept. They would have some respite from the cramped quarters and heaving of the ships. The children were excited. Taking a few items of personal gear with them, the Pilgrim families walked the third of a mile from the quay to the almost completed building.

It was soon obvious to the shipwrights that the *Speedwell* was over-masted and giving too much sail. The lengthy vertical

David Thomson: First Yankee

lever (mast) laboring in the wind tended to loosen the seams between the strakes. Water pressure would force out the oakum calking and cause leaks. The answer? Refit the vessel with a shorter mast and use a smaller sail.

It was equally obvious that the master and crew of the *Speedwell* fully intended to back out of their agreement to serve the Pilgrims in America for a year. They would not go to America under any circumstances.

While the Brownist leaders labored with the problems of what to do, the women and children reveled in their relative comfort at the Orphans' Aid workhouse. Six months pregnant, Amias Cole and her two children, Prissilla nearly four years old and John twenty months, visited the newcomers at Orphans' Aid. Amias told stories to the Brownist children and talked to the women about New England, Indians and ships, giving them some encouragement. Amias stated that she hoped to cross the sea in a few years.

At the end of August, a small, unofficial group of travelers, including Miles Standish, William Bradford and the master of the *Mayflower*, Captain Christopher Jones, called upon David Thomson in the Captain's House at Plymouth Fort. Thomson was at the Fort frequently to take care of Commander Gorges' personal affairs during the knight's absence to London. The *Mayflower* men sought out David Thomson to learn from him what they could about America. They had copies of Captain John Smith's *Map and Description of New England* which had been published a few years before. Captain Jones explained that the destination of the migration ostensibly was on the American mainland around forty degrees latitude, several leagues south of Hudson's River. The Brownists had a patent from the south Virginia (Jamestown) Company for that area. They had not been able to get much information about the territory of their grant.

David Thomson: First Yankee

Thomas Weston and Captain John Smith in London had recommended to the Brownists that they consider going to New England. However, when this idea was proposed to members of the expedition, it met some favor, but also started many arguments. Besides, they learned that Sir Ferdinando Gorges did not yet have his charter and hence could not give the Brownists a patent for land in New England. They could not wait for a patent. They were too far committed. They must get to America.

Thomson told the group he had never been to Hudson's River, let alone south of it. He had only been a few leagues south and west of the big hook of Cape Cod which Captain Smith called Cape James on his map. Thomson said he understood that Hudson's River must be about twenty leagues south of Cape Cod's latitude and at least fifty leagues further west. He understood that the Dutch had something going around the mouth of Hudson's River although the English claimed that territory.

Thomson was asked what he thought about the feasibility of the Brownists going to New England to plant instead of going to Virginia. Thomson's reply was that he could make no judgement about the area for which they had a patent. He did not know anyone in Plymouth who had been in that part of Virginia. As for New England, he had been there several times and thought it to be a place of great promise. He thought that if the Brownists should choose to go to New England, they would have no trouble getting a land patent from the soon to be Council for the Settlement of New England, especially if they were already there. Sir Ferdinando Gorges was the leader in the proposed Council. Thomson thought that if the Brownists were seated in New England, Sir Ferdinando would not expel them.

Thomson was asked where he thought would be a good place to investigate if the Brownist settlers should want to

David Thomson: First Yankee

consider going to New England instead of Virginia. Thomson told the group that he had recently received a communication from Captain Thomas Dermer in New England via a Plymouth fishing vessel. The letter was a report from Dermer to Sir Ferdinando Gorges and was dated June 30, just two months ago. Thomson had made a copy of the report and had then forwarded the original to Gorges who was in London. Thomson produced his copy and read parts of it to the conferees.

In it, Dermer recommended to Gorges that if the first plantation to New England numbered more than fifty persons, it should be seated at the place which is called Plymouth on Captain John Smith's map. But if there should be less that fifty persons in the expedition, then they should plant near the mouth of the Charles River in Massachusetts Bay some nine leagues north of Plymouth. Thomson said he agreed with Dermer's judgement. In fact, Dermer and Thomson had discussed the matter and reached the same opinion when they were together on the spot in New England in 1619.

The conferees were greatly interested in the contents of Demer's report and asked Thomson many questions about Plymouth and Charlton. Thomson had visited both places in 1616 with Vines and again in 1619 with Dermer. He told the group that he expected eventually to have a trading post on 'his' island in Massachusetts Bay.

Captain Jones, who had not been to New England before but had engaged in whaling in Greenland, asked about the best route to take to go to Cape Cod since the emigrants were likely to go there whether they stopped there or not. Cape Cod was on the way to Virginia anyway.

Thomson suggested that when he got past Land's End (England), Captain Jones should try to make good compass course of west-northwest, two points north of west on the

David Thomson: First Yankee

compass, for about four hundred leagues. The course would take them along between 51 degrees and 52 degrees latitude. The compass variation will slowly increase from 10 degrees west to 25 or 26 degrees west. When he came to where the variation was 25 degrees west and he was around 51 degrees latitude, he should shift his course a little to port to compass west. This will move the ship southwesterly more or less parallel to the coast. When the vessel gets to 42 degrees latitude, he should shift to true west and aim to ride the forty-second parallel right in to Cape Cod or Cape James on Smith's map.

The delegation was pleased with the information about New England given to them by David Thomson. They agreed that Plimouth sounded like a good place to consider for their plantation. However, they decided that it was better to tell only a few expedition leaders about what they had learned from David Thomson and let the leaders come to a decision before getting the rank and file of emigrants stirred up about a possible change in their destination.

The Brownist leaders eventually realized that the skipper and crew of the *Speedwell* would not go to America under any circumstance. Hence a major overhaul of the *Speedwell* was not justifiable. They did not have the time. It was decided to 'dismiss' the pinnace and part their company and proceed with only the *Mayflower*.

They transferred from the *Speedwell* to the *Mayflower* all the provisions they could. The chose some twenty-five people to leave behind, including those who wanted to drop out and those "...thought least useful and most unfit to bear the brunt of this hard adventure."

After twelve days in the hospitable port of Plymouth, the Mayflower, with its 102 passengers, set sail again on Wednesday, September 6, 1620. Half of them would not live to see another September roll around. The Thomsons would meet some of the survivors in America in less than three years.

November 1620: Gorges gets his Charter

When the Brownist pilgrims were in Plymouth, Sir Ferdinando Gorges was still in London defending his proposed charter for a Council for New England from assaults by Virginia, fishermen, M.P.'s and others.

Despite opposition, the Charter of the Council for New England passed the seals on November 3, 1620. The charter incorporated a group of forty aristocrats to be the governing body. Their names "...read like an abstract from peerage." Seven of them were members of the King's Privy Council. The Council was to be self-perpetuating. Sir Ferdinando Gorges was the dominating member throughout the Council's brief existence. In fact, it was said of him that he "was the Council."

The charter gave the Council complete power over all affairs in New England. It could award land, set up governments, enact and enforce laws, grant licenses and tax commercial enterprises and appoint officials. Immediately after its creation, the Council for New England's sweeping power began to be eroded. It lasted fifteen years. Less than a dozen of the original forty council members ever manifested any interest in the council.

Gorges' general plan was that two parts of New England should be divided among the aristocratic members of the Council. These members would in turn make sub grants of land, establish settlements and set up local governments within their plantations. A third part of New England was to remain in the possession of the Council to be developed as a public plantation.

David Thomson: First Yankee

Grants were to be made to individuals or groups who set up towns in the public domain to provide a reservoir or workmen and where industries would develop. The whole territory, public and private, would come under the control of a governor appointed by the Council for New England. The governor would carry out the laws passed by an assembly of legislators elected from all the parts of the colony.

Thus, the first two parts of the colony would be composed of great plantations in the hands of aristocrats, while the public plantation would be settled by craftsmen, tradesmen and merchants who would develop cities where guildsmen would control the municipal affairs as in England. The colonial legislature would be dominated by Council members or their agents. Sir Ferdinando expected to be the first resident Governor of New England.

The aristocratic landowners of the great plantations would largely finance themselves until their plantations became self-supporting. The public settlements would be financed by wealthy English merchants who would develop trade with the new world: and by skilled craftsmen and artisans who could largely support themselves shortly after their arrival; and by English cities which could subsidize their able poor to get to New England where they would soon become self-supporting; and by taxes on fishing ships and other income producing commerce. It was a grandiose scheme. It did not work.

During the first nineteen months of its existence, Gorges with a few intimates on the Council for New England, conducted affairs of the Council with casual informality. Few, if any, records were kept. Many actions were taken based on agreements between gentlemen whose words were their bonds. Contracts about money and series were settled by a nod or a handshake. Some patents for land were written out but never acted upon. It is likely that some were agreed upon and acted upon but never written. There is indication that some patents were written long after the oral commitment had been made and the implementing action had been taken.

Although many of his actions may seem to be high-handed, Gorges did not seek his own aggrandizement. A nobleman by birth, he felt it was his duty to do what, in his judgment, was best for his king, country and people. Noblesse oblige. Gorges was a man of impeccable integrity. He was a life-long professional military man possessing a strict code of honor. He was a natural commanding officer who gained and held the respect of all those who served under him. He was a model Elizabethan nobleman. His associates on the Council for New England were agreeable to following, without question, his dynamic and autocratic leadership from a distance – and let him do all the work.

As soon as the charter for the Council for New England passed the seals on November 3, 1620, Sir Ferdinando took some steps to move ahead on his plans for colonization of New England. He hoped to be able to go to New England himself as governor in 1622. Four things needed to be done:

1. Money, capital, must be recruited to sustain the enterprise until it could become self-supporting or even income producing. This problem was never adequately solved. However, several Council members contributed one hundred pounds each to the cause. Most did not.

2. The council should have a large ship at its disposal for the transportation of colonists, supplies and produce. It should be equipped for fishing and for the defense of the coast and coastal traffic. Construction of the large ship, *Great Neptune*, 534 tons, and a pinnace escort was started in 1620-1621 at Whitby in Yorkshire. Hopefully it would be ready in 1622. Construction

was slowed by lack of funds. The ship was not finished until 1624 and then it was subject to litigation. It participated in the war with Spain. It never got to America.

3. An operating base, a fort, should be built and armed in New England to be ready for the governor when he should arrive, hopefully in 1622. David Thomson and a crew of builders was sent in Plymouth fishing vessels to Pascataway in early 1621. They built Pannaway Fort. Ordinance for the fort was sent over in 1622.

4. A detailed plan should be devised and publicized for the orderly settlement of New England and the appropriate government thereof. This was formulated. Gorges published it in 1622 entitled, *A Brief Relation of the Discovery Plantation of New England: the Climb and Condition of the Country, and the Present Estate of our Affairs There; The Platform of the Government, and Division of the Territories in General.*

New Hampshire 1621-1625
1621 Expedition to Isles of Shoals and Pascataway

When the charter establishing the Council for New England passed the seals, November 3, 1620, Sir Ferdinando in London sent word to his servant, David Thomson in Plymouth, to go ahead with their plan to construct a fort for Gorges at the mouth of the Piscataqua River in New England. The arrangement was to have Plymouth merchants provide transportation to Pascataway on fishing vessels for Thomson and his construction crew with their tools and supplies. In return, the merchant would receive the right to fish for the season around the Isles of Shoals. They could establish a fishing station at Pascataway. They could use Gorges' fort to house their wintering fishermen

David Thomson: First Yankee

during the first winter, 1621-1622. It was understood that Gorges would eventually issue a patent to David Thomson and the Plymouth merchants to validate the understanding.

Although the Plymouth merchants intended to fight Gorges' authority to tax fishing in New England with any means available to them; they were not averse to helping their neighbor, Gorges, to advance his other plans for New England. The fishermen were pleased with the prospect of having the security of a fort near their fishing center at the Isles of Shoals.

Preparations for joining the fort building expedition with the fishing voyages were already underway when David Thomson received the go ahead from Gorges. Plymouth merchants fully intended to send fishing vessels to New England in 1621 whether or not Gorges' charter was approved. They had started their preparations for the new fishing season. The fort builders were just a little extra cargo.

The merchants planned to send two ships to the Isles of Shoals in 1621. The first one would leave Plymouth in December, 1620. It would take fishermen to the Isles of Shoals. They would get the previously constructed fishing stages, drying racks and boats at the Isles of Shoals ready for the new season. Then they would start fishing. David Thomson and an advance construction crew would go on this ship. Their job would be to help the fishing get started at the Isles and then move to the mainland. There they would lay out the work for building Gorges' fort.

That first ship would remain at the Isles of Shoals for only a brief time. It would then proceed to Monhegan Island and load a cargo of fish which had been caught and processed in the preceding fall season by fishermen permanently stationed there.

About the end of January, the Plymouth merchants would dispatch a second vessel from Plymouth for Pascataway with

David Thomson: First Yankee

supplies and gear and a few more fishermen-builders. This ship would remain at Pascataway until June when a full load of fish would be ready to take to market.

A team of fishermen-builders would be left at Pascataway for a year to work on fort construction. They would fish during the fall season and again in the spring. They would spend the winter working on the fort under David Thomson's direction.

Thereafter, Plymouth ships would call regularly at the Isles of Shoals and Pascataway in June and December to pick up the spring and fall catches, and to bring in supplies and personnel.

Sometime in late December 1620, David bade Amias, Priscilla and John good-bye. He boarded the *Jonathan* with his construction crew to sail to the new world. Many of the fishermen and sailors on board were his friends and neighbors in Plymouth.

The ship took the usual northern sailing route to New England. The voyagers were out of sight of land from Land's End (England) until the Isles of Shoals and the main were sighted. Eight weeks were taken in the crossing. Most of the fishermen were put ashore at the Isles to commence their work.

The *Jonathan*, with Thomson and some construction workers, proceeded to the mainland near Odiorne's Point and anchored. The men got ready to lighter men and equipment to shore.

Some Indians were waiting on the beach when the *Jonathan* dropped anchor. They had seen the vessel coming from the Isles and knew it was a fishing ship. The natives had watched it until they guessed where it was going to heave to and then they ran to meet it. They were excited. It was not the novelty of the ship that excited them, they had seen many such. The newcomers soon learned the cause of the natives' agitation.

It seems that rumors were fast spreading among the Indians

David Thomson: First Yankee

that a large ship loaded with white people, including women and children, had put in at Cape Cod. The Indians did not know the nationality of the pale faces. They were neither fishermen nor traders. Groups of armed men from this ship would go ashore form time to time and tramp among the sand dunes, digging into Indian graves, stealing cached Indian seed corn. They desecrated an Indian cemetery and robbed some vacated Indian dwellings. When the white men saw an Indian, they chased him. There had been a skirmish between the whites and the reds but there were no casualties, yet.

The Plymothians on the *Jonathan* realized that the newcomers at Cape Cod must be those Brownists who had left Plymouth the previous September on the *Mayflower* to go to America to make a new home for themselves where they could practice their own religion and keep their children free of the sinful world.

David Thomson, the skipper of the *Jonathan* and a few other white leaders at Pascataway conferred concerning what, if anything, should be done to defuse the tension existing at Cape Cod. It was decided that they should send a couple of men in a shallop back to the Isles of Shoals to notify their fishermen colleagues there of the potential Indian problem at Cape Cod. Then these messengers would proceed on to Monhegan Island and apprise their compatriots there of the explosive situation at Accomack. They were to recommend to their Monhegan associates that they consult with Indian Sagamore Unnongoit (the English called him Captain John Somerset or just Somerset) and try to induce him to go to Cape Cod and try to bring the Brownists and Indians tougher in peace.

On learning the situation at Cape Cod, the Plymouth fishermen at Monhegan immediately got in touch with Somerset who had counselled with Captain Dermer during Dermer's and

David Thomson: First Yankee

Squanto's peace and goodwill efforts in the summers of 1619 and 1620.

Somerset volunteered to go to Accomack and try to bring the races together. Fishermen sailed Somerset to Massachusetts Bay where they set him ashore. They wished him good luck on his mission to Accomack. In one week, Somerset had established good relations between the Pilgrims and their Indian neighbors. He brought Squanto to the Pilgrims to be their interpreter.

Back at Pascataway, David Thomson explained to the Indians that the white immigrants at Cape Cod were English and that they meant no harm. They were just ignorant. He said he would try to find a way of instructing the Cape Cod white people how to cooperate with their Indian neighbors. The Pascataway Indians were sternly reminded that things must not get out of hand at Cape Cod. It might result in a tragic race war. The Plymouth fishermen at Pascataway hoped that this information would quickly drift back along the Indian grapevine to Cape Cod and cool things off until Somerset could get there.

While expedition leaders were discussing what should be done about the Brownist-Indian confrontation to Accomack, other men were busy lightering supplies, tools and gear ashore from the *Jonathan* to the beach at Odiorne's Point. When the task was completed, the *Jonathan* returned to the Isles of Shoals. Soon thereafter, the *Jonathan* went on to Monhegan where a cargo of fish caught the previous fall by Plymouth fishermen was ready to be taken to markets in England.

The first task of the construction crew at Pascataway was to choose a site for the fort. Gorges' instructions were clear. He wanted the fort built so it would dominate the two mouths of the Piscataqua River with long range cannons, thus denying the use of the river to any potential European enemy. The fort must also be able to withstand a land attack from red or white foe.

The site chosen for the fort was on a rise of ground overlooking the mouths of the river. Supplies and equipment were moved from the beach to the site. The red men were curious to know what their white brethren were doing. They were told that the English were going to build a fort and headquarters for a great English Sachem. The Indians marveled at the saws, axes and other iron tools which the Englishmen used.

Thomson arranged with the Indians to provide the white men with fresh meat, game and fowl - and such grains, nuts, corn or herbs that they might have available. Fishermen at the Isles kept the Pascataway construction crew supplied with fresh fish.

In April, the *Providence* arrived from Plymouth with more supplies and personnel. At the end of the fishing season in June, the *Providence* loaded up with fish at the Isles of Shoals and departed for England. Some of the fishermen returned to Plymouth on the *Providence*. Those fort builders and fishermen who were to remain at Pascataway during the summer and winter sent messages home to Plymouth on the *Providence*.

During the summer slack time between the spring and fall fishing seasons, a few of the fishermen stayed on the Isles of shoals doing repair and maintenance work on the fishing facilities there. More of the fishermen joined Thomson and the construction crew to help with the fort building. A few cleared land for a garden, having already given instructions to their homeward bound shipmates to bring or send seeds when a ship came back to Pascataway in the winter.

By fall, there was a substantial structure in being at Pannaway. It was nearly ready to receive armament which was to be sent over from London in the spring of 1622. In September, those men whose principal job was fishing, returned to the Isles of Shoals and renewed their harvesting of fish. Thomson's crew continued to work on Gorges' fort. As autumn advanced, preparations were made for winter when Pannaway was to house not only the construction crew but also the fishermen from the Isles of Shoals.

There was a large shelter and adequate food for winter. Plenty of wood fuel was ready for the fireplaces and more was available. The Englishmen were well armed, although the Indians presented no threat. Ninety percent of the Indians had died during the previous few years. The danger of hostilities breaking out at New Plymouth between the Brownists and the Indians had faded. There was plenty of work to be done to keep the men busy.

The *Jonathan* returned to Pascataway in January 1622, with supplies and news from home for the fishermen and construction crew. After a few days, the *Jonathan* went to the Isles of Shoals to pick up a load of fish which the Plymouth fishermen had caught and processed in the fall season. On board the *Jonathan* for the return voyage to England was David Thomson and a few of his crew. Thomson was returning to Plymouth at the behest of his patron, Sir Ferdinando Gorges. Most of the construction crew and fishermen remained at Pascataway to continue their work.

We have no detailed information about the structure of the fort beyond that provided by Samuel Maverick who was there in 1623 and many times thereafter. wrote that the fort was "...a strong and large house, enclosed with a large and high Falizado and mounted guns..." The building probably had a stone foundation with a two story superstructure of logs and boards. That the building was large is confirmed by the fact that there must have been at least thirty people entertained there for months during the winter of 1623-1624. The builders had the capabilities of hand sawing and splitting boards from logs. David Thomson and his crew had considerable experience in building construction with wood and stone in Plymouth.

Pascataway

Pascataway was a name in common use in the early seventeenth century for the area around the estuary of the Piscataqua River[5]. It was soon applied to the scattered settlements of English who planted there.

In November 1622, David Thomson received a patent for six thousand acres from the Council for New England. The grant extended from Fox Point along the southwest bank of the River and four miles down the Atlantic shore. It included the six hundred acre Great Island. Thomson became a partner with three Plymouth merchants by designating Great Island as a fishing base for Plymouth fishermen.

From 1624 to 1629, Gorges and leading members of the Council for New England were preoccupied with martial duties in England's wars with Spain and France. Activity at Pannaway Fort slackened. David Thomson moved to 'his' island in Massachusetts Bay. The population of the small fishing village at Pascataway Harbor slowly increased. Fishing at the Isles of Shoals continued unabated.

England's wars over in 1629, Gorges and colleagues revived their interest in New England. They believed that the Piscataqua River came from interior lakes and would therefore be a water

---

[5] The Piscataqua River forms part of the boundary between New Hampshire and Maine.

highway to lucrative Indian trade there. They formed the Laconia Company in 1629. They took over Pannaway Fort and then moved up river and started a settlement at Strawbery Banke, where there was a deep water port. It was a base for the Laconia Company. Strawbery Banke eventually became Portsmouth, NH.

1621-1622 Gorges in Plymouth and London

When David Thomson left Plymouth for Pascataway at the end of December 1620, Sir Ferdinando's hopes for a royal charter establishing a Council for New England had already been stalled for nearly a year. His request for a charter had been submitted March 3, 1619. It had passed the seals November 3, 1620 but had been held 'undelivered.' Finally, after Parliament had adjourned for the summer, the Privy Council ordered the Charter for the Council for New England delivered June 18, 1621.

Although Gorges had been handicapped by not having possession of the charter, he had moved ahead with some of his plans for New England, such as starting the construction of the *Great Neptune* and a pinnace at Whitby, and having Thomson build a fort at Pascataway. Within a month after the *Mayflower* returned to London, and eighteen days before the charter was delivered, Gorges had issued the Pilgrims a patent for land in New England thus legalizing their occupation of New Plymouth. However, the long frustrating delay of the charter had dashed Gorges' original hopes of being able to go to New England in 1622. Progress on the *Great Neptune* was stalled for lack of money. The Council was little more than a list of names on paper rather than a dynamic body. They had never been organized.

David Thomson: First Yankee

At the beginning of summer, 1621, Gorges went back to Plymouth from London. Some of the new Council members lived in the west and he wanted to get them on the job. But perhaps a more pressing reason was because international tensions had been increasing – war with Spain and possibly France seemed imminent and he had to return to his post as Governor of Plymouth Fort. His military responsibilities for preparing the fort and regional defenses for possible war took much of his time and energy and money.

Plymouth fishing vessels returning from the Isles of Shoals and Pascataway in the late summer reported to Gorges that satisfactory progress was being made on the fort and that it would be ready to receive ordnance in late spring of 1622.

Toward the end of 1621, the threat of war diminished. Sir Ferdinando was eager to get back to promoting settlement of New England. About this time, his son, Captain Robert Gorges, returned to Plymouth from the Venetian wars. Sir Ferdinando designated Robert deputy commander of Plymouth Fort and left him in charge while the knight moved to London.

December 21, 1621, widower Sir Ferdinando Gorges married Mary Fulford, widow of Thomas Achim. This brought him some welcome money.

Sir Ferdinando Gorges and his bride, Lady Mary, and some servants moved into the Gorges' town house in Clerkenwell (London) in January 1622. Gorges intended to make a supreme effort to advance the settlement of New England this year.

One of his first tasks was to arrange for some ordnance to be sent over form London Arsenal to the newly built fort at Pascataway. He sought the assistance of friends on the Privy Council, some of whom were also members of the Council for New England. His efforts brought results. Listed in the *Acts of the Privy Council of England, 1621-1623*, in the Public Record

David Thomson: First Yankee

Office, London, is a letter from the Privy Council to Lord Carew, Master of Ordnance, dated February 17, 1622, directing him on behalf of the Council of New England to grant a license to Thomas Weston, merchant of London, to send over to New England in the ship *Charity*, or any other ship, thirty pieces of iron ordnance, namely fifteen demi-culverins (long range guns), weighing 1.5 to 1.8 tons each; ten sakers weighing 1.o to 1.4 tons each; and five minions, 0.7 to 1.0 tons, totaling over forty tons.

Two patents for land were issued in the name of the Council for New England in 1622. Their issuance gives clues to intentions relative to New England at the time although there was little or no action taken to implement the land grants.

On March 9, 1622, a patent was issued to Captain John Mason conveying to him all the land lying between the Naumkeag (Salem, Massachusetts) and the Merrimac Rivers. The area included Cape Ann on the coast. The extensive tract was called Mariana. Ambrose Gibbons, a servant of Mason was designated to put Captain Mason in possession.

Some historians speculate that Ambrose Gibbons may have been in New England in 1622. If so, he may have been left in charge of the newly built Pannaway Fort when David Thomson departed for England in January 1621.

August 10, 1622, the Council made a grant to Gorges and Mason jointly of land lying upon the sea coast between the Merrimac and Kennebec Rivers extending sixty miles into the country. This was called the Province of Maine. It also included what is now New Hampshire. A provision in the Maine patent states:

"…that the said Sir Ferdinando Gorges and Captain John Mason shall and will before the expiration of three years from the date here-of, have in or upon the said portions of lands or some part thereof, one part with a competent guard and ten families at least of his majesty's subjects resident and being in and upon the said premises or in default thereof shall and will forfeit one hundred pounds."

The two patents mark the beginning of the close relationship between Sir Ferdinando Gorges and Captain John Mason.

The requirement that Gorges and Mason have a 'competent guard' and at least ten families settled in Maine before 1625 may have had reference to Pannaway Fort where just such a settlement and competent guard was already in the process of being developed by Thomson. As yet there were no families, but there would be.

In the spring of 1622, Gorges decided that the activities of the Council for New England should be put on a more businesslike basis. Up to this time, he had been endeavoring with some success to get things started by private negotiations and personal contacts. Now he wanted to marshal his forces and move forward on a broad front to accelerate settlement of New England. To this end, he decided that the Council for New England should have regular, formal meetings and keep formal records. There are records of meetings of the Council from May 31, 1622 through June of 1623.

During the thirteen months, thirty-seven meetings of the Council were reported. Probably all of them were held in London. David Thomson attended at least six of them.

The 'minutes' of the meetings, if they may be called that, are sketchy and incomplete. They read more like informal memoranda of some of the actions taken at some of the meetings of the Council. The names of the Council present at each session are listed. The number ranges from two to seven with an average of 4.4. Sir Ferdinando was absent from only one meeting. Eight Council members attended only once in thirty-seven meetings.

David Thomson: First Yankee

Only five members attended more than ten times. Twenty-four different Council members are listed as attending at least once. The authorized membership of the Council was forty.

The Council for New England was ineffective. It continued to be a one-man show. The few able noblemen on the Council had other responsibilities and did not have much time to help Gorges. The fight for free fishing which raged for two years in and out of Commons against the Council for New England's authority to license fishing, discouraged eligible noblemen from being identified with the Council. Few were eager to pay the one hundred pounds for "membership dues."

Spring 1622: Thomson Back in Plymouth

David Thomson arrived in Plymouth from Pascataway on the *Jonathan* in March 1622. He joined his family at his home on White Cross Street. He had been away more than a year building Fort Pannaway for Gorges. It was a happy reunion. Prissilla was now five and a half and John was two and a half.

Thomson sent word to Gorges in London about the progress on the fort and the situation at Pascataway. The fort was ready to receive ordinance at any time. Relations with the Indians were good. Fishing around the Isles of Shoals had been a commercial success. The shore based facilities for processing fish at the Isles of Shoals had been expanded. Some Plymouth fishermen spent the winter at the fort. They were probably fishing now. Thomson told Gorges that he and his wife, Amias, were still desirous of going to New England at the appropriate time. Thomson said he was at Gorges' command.

Thomson also reported to the Plymouth merchants who had made the fort building expedition possible. The merchants were pleased with the success of their fishing vessels around the Isles of Shoals. Thomson learned that the merchants of Plymouth and other west England towns were marshaling their forces to try to eliminate Gorges' authority to tax New England fishing.

For a few weeks, David helped his father-in-law in shipwright work. He and Amias visited some of their friends. David called upon Captain Robert Gorges, a boyhood friend, at Plymouth Fort. Robert was acting as commander or Governor of Plymouth Fort as a deputy for his father, Sir Ferdinando, who was in London. Young Gorges lived in the Captain's House at the Fort.

June-July 1622: Thomson in London

In May 1622, Thomson received a request from Gorges to report to the capital. Arriving on the Thames in June, Thomson walked to the Gorges home in Clerkenwell where Sir Ferdinando was living with his new wife. When he was a boy, David had often been in this house where his father had been a steward. Now his old friend and tutor from Plymouth, Dr. Richard Vines, was household manager for Gorges. Dr. Vines warmly greeted his former apprentice.

During his sojourn in London, Thomson lived with the Gorgeses. He acted as private secretary and alter ego for the knight. He learned that Sir Ferdinando was writing a brochure about New England and wanted David to help with the last part in which he discussed "The Climb and Condition of the Country, and the present estate of our affairs there."

The Gorgeses sometimes entertained noble friends in their home when David Thomson was present. Londoners were very interested in the new world. Thomson was well informed about New England. Gorges' noble guests would listen attentively to Thomson tell about his experiences in America. To sir Ferdinando's disappointment, few of his friends evinced any interest in investing money in his projects for settling New England.

Three meetings of the Council for New England were held in London during July 1622. David attended with Sir Ferdinando. Lack of interest by Council members is indicated by the fact that only four of the forty councilors were present for two of the meetings and only three answered the roll for the other one. Gorges was the only councilor to attend all three meetings.

At the July 5 meeting, David Thomson was delegated to attend the King's Privy Council "…with a petition to his Majesty for forfeits committed by Thomas Weston. As also to solicit ye Lords for procuring from his Majesty a proclamation concerning ye fishermen of ye western parts. Likewise to procure some course for punishing their contempt of authority…"

It is not clear just what Weston's crime was except that it probably had to do with the thirty cannon he had been authorized to transport to New England in the spring. He may have sold some of the cannon and pocketed the cash. In any case most, if not all, of the cannon arrived at Pascataway in the summer of 1622.

David Thomson was aware of the lawless practices of some of the English fishermen in New England: stealing one another's fishing equipment, wantonly destroying trees and cheating Indians. He was an appropriate agent to take the issue to the Privy Council on behalf of the Council for New England.

The 'minutes' of the "Wednesday ye 24th of July 1622" meeting has this entry: "Mr. Thomson is appointed to attend the

Lords (of the Privy Council) for a warrant to Mr. Attorney General for drawing ye new patent and Sir Henry Spilman is desired to attend Mr. Attorney thereabouts."

The Council for New England wanted a new charter or an amendment from the Crown which would give the Council greater authority over the nature of the land tenures which it could grant in New England. They also desired "That there may be power given to the (charter) to create Titles of Honor and precedency so as they differ in nomination from the titles used here in England."

Late Summer 1622

During the three months, July 24 to October 22, 1622, only one meeting of the Council for New England was held. That was on August 6. It was the only meeting of the twenty-seven held during the year 1622-1623 which Gorges did not attend. It is our opinion that after the July 24 meeting of the Council, Sir Ferdinando left London to go to the west country to consult with the Council members whose zeal was flagging, if it ever existed. He hoped to get new converts to his schemes for New England. Gorges took with him his secretary and protégé, David Thomson.

An early stop on their trip west was at Portsmouth, Hampshire, where Captain John Mason had his base and home. (Mason had returned from Newfoundland in 1621.) Mason and Gorges worked on strategy and tactics to use to promote settlement of New England. Probably it was at this time, August 10, 1622, that Gorges and Mason drafted the Province of Maine Charter (supra).

There is no record that this Maine patent was implemented

immediately but it must have played a part in the thinking and actions of the persons involved in the summer and fall of 1622. We can imagine Gorges and Mason discussing New England problems at Portsmouth with David Thomson listening in.

Perhaps it was at Portsmouth, Hampshire, August 1622, that Gorges and mason agreed that David Thomson was to be given a sub-grant of 6000 acres of land along the Piscataqua River in the province of Maine which would include the fort which Thomson had recently built for Gorges. On this land they hoped that a city would be developed with a population composed of craftsmen, artisans, merchants, laborers, etc. The guildsmen of the city would have authority to make regulations controlling affairs of the city similar to the situation which prevailed in the cities of England. Gorges, Mason and the noblemen of the Council for New England, representing the Crown, would have ultimate jurisdiction over the provincial government of Maine.

Gorges and Mason would keep title to Pannaway Fort but Thomson could use it until the proprietors had need for it either for defense or as a temporal provincial headquarters. In the meantime, Thomson could profit from the fishing through his association with the Plymouth merchants. He could build a trading post in some suitable location, perhaps at the strawberry banks along the river just above where the two mouths of the river divided. There was a deep-water port there. It was desirable to have a deep-water port near the mouth of the river leading to the interior where boats used in inland trade could meet oceangoing ships. Mason liked the idea of calling the proposed city at the mouth of the river Portsmouth, after his home city in Hampshire.

After their satisfactory conference with Captain Mason, Sir Ferdinando and David left Portsmouth. Gorges had other men

David Thomson: First Yankee

to see. Thomson headed for Plymouth to be with his family and friends and to prepare for going to Pascataway with his family early next year. Gorges requested David to report back to London in October to be of assistance to Gorges and the Council for New England.

Arriving in Plymouth in late August, 1622, David Thomson immediately went home to his family. He told Amias that it was fairly certain that the family would be leaving for New England in January to make their permanent home. The Coles, father and stepmother of Amias who lived next door, took the news rather hard although they had been expecting such for years.

It was decided that six-year-old Prissilla would stay in Plymouth with her grandparents for a few years, but that four-year-old John would accompany his parents to the new world. Since David was to leave to return to duty in London in October, there was much to be done in the intervening five or six weeks.

One of the first things David Thomson did after arriving in Plymouth from Portsmouth was to consult with Plymouth merchants who earlier had tentatively agreed to invest in Thomson's New England enterprise in return for securing fishing privileges. Thomson told the merchants that Gorges had agreed to give him a patent for six thousand acres of land on the Piscataqua River. Thomson wanted to use this land as collateral for the merchants' financial support. Three members of the Plymouth merchants' guild, Abraham Colmer, Nicholas Sherwill and Leonard Pomeroy, were designated to enter into a contract with Thomson when he shall have received his patent from the Council for New England.

The merchants wanted control over a few hundred acres of land on the mainland where they could have a fishing staging and a permanent fishing village not too far from the principal fishing center at the Isles of Shoals. They could not expect their

David Thomson: First Yankee

fishermen to winter at Fort Pannaway any longer. Great Island, a little over six hundred acres, was the tract selected.

The fishing station and settlement would be at deep Pascataway Harbor on the east side of Great Island. For five years, the four parties: Thomson, Colmer, Sherwill and Pomeroy, would share the expense of developing the fishing station and its hinterland. Before the end of five years, the six hundred acres and all improvements thereon were to be divided equally into four parts and each partner to get one part. Thus the three Plymouth merchants would ultimately hold the controlling interest in the station and settlement at Pascataway Harbor. Profits resulting from the fishing there were to be shared according to each partner's annual investment in the fishing venture. David Thomson could invest in fishing to the extent that he wished up to one-fourth for any particular season.

The four partners would share in the cost of sending a building crew of seven men to Pascataway in 1623. David Thomson was to direct these men in erecting habitations at a fishing settlement for year-round living quarters for fishermen and their families.

As for the balance of the six thousand acres, Thomson was to pay three-fourths of the cost of improvement and receive three-fourths of the profits resulting therefrom. By the end of five years, the five thousand, four hundred acres were to be divided with three fourths going to Thomson and one-fourth to the three merchants.

During his five or six weeks in Plymouth in the late summer of 1622, David Thomson gave some consideration to the matter of the personnel to accompany him to Pascataway in January of 1623. He planned to take a few servants, male and female, to help him and Amias with household and business affairs. Then there was the selection of the seven men who were to act as

David Thomson: First Yankee

builders for the habitations at the fishing station. Thomson expected to recruit some persons to go to New England aboard English fishing vessels who would indenture themselves to the Council for New England for two years' service. They would work under Thomson, agent for the Council. For transporting the indentured servants, the Council for New England would permit ship owners' crews to fish for the season.

It is also possible that David was to arrange for the transportation of the families of one or two men who had gone with him to Pascataway to build Pannaway Fort in 1621 and were still there.

Thomson expected to maintain Gorges' fort for his patron for a year or two until Sir Ferdinando could arrive on the scene to take over. In the meantime, Thomson would set up his trading post on his six thousand acres near the fort or up the river at the deep water port where the river divided to form Great Island. He would need a stock of trading goods. This would take some planning.

Fall 1622

David Thomson in Plymouth was well along with his preparations to go to America when it was time for him to return to London in accordance with his arrangement with Sir Ferdinando. Toward the end of October, 1622, David arrived in Clerkenwell.

Sir Ferdinando had returned to London a few weeks before Thomson's arrival. Gorges had not had much luck recruiting financial support for his Council for New England in his swing through the West Country. In London, Gorges had started convening meetings of the Council. The response of the councilmen was poor. In addition to Gorges, only two members attended the meetings with any regularity. They were the treasurer, Dr. Barnabe Gooch, Dean of Exeter; and Naval Captain Sir Samuel Argall (who had been active in the Jamestown settlement; had destroyed the French settlement in Maine in 1613; had transported Pocahontas and her companions to Plymouth and London in 1616; and now was much interested in promoting settlement of New England.) The low attendance at the meetings of the Council did not deter Gorges from conducting council business and making decisions outside of meetings where no records were kept.

About this time, Sir Ferdinando was plagued with another problem. In October, 1622, his son, Robert, whom he had left in Plymouth acting as deputy commander of the Fort, attempted to seize a French Catholic ship which had run aground near Plymouth. Robert intended to award the vessel to de Soubise, a protestant leader in the French civil war. Justice of the Peace, Sir Thomas Wise, near whose land the ship was stranded, opposed the move whereupon hot headed Robert attempted to arrest Sir Thomas. Robert's distorted report of the incident led to an investigation by the Lords of the King's Privy Council. Justice of the Peace Wise was completely exonerated and the blame was laid on young Gorges. Robert was strongly reprimanded by the Lords. He was commanded to apologize. "...their Lordships having been pleased in regard of his father (forbore to inflict) further punishment upon him, although his offense doth merit a more severe censure." This episode may have been a factor in the immediate commencement of behind the scenes arrangements for Robert to go to America.

Fifteen meetings of the Council for New England were held between October 22 and December 17, 1622. Evidently, David Thomson was present at five of the meetings in November and

David Thomson: First Yankee

December. He may have attended a few others.

From the 'minutes' we learn that Gorges and a few faithful colleagues sought to push the construction of the Council's large ship, *Great Neptune*, being built at Whitby. They were constantly frustrated by lack of money.

They worked on details for a new royal charter of the Council which would give it more power to set up governments in New England and authority to issue patents with more options for grantees to transfer title land.

The Council sought ways of painlessly and lucratively taxing fishing to subsidize settlement. They adopted a policy whereby fishing ships could receive the right to fish for the season in exchange for transporting prospective settlers. An entry in the 'minutes' for November 16 reads, "It is thought fit to contract with ye merchants to carry for every thirty tons or under one man, if the ship be fifty ton or upwards, under sixty, which is two parts of three, then to carry two men and so proportionally; and to leave those men in New England, victualled for two months...If they refuse to carry men, then demand ten pounds for every thirty tons or under and so ratably...."

The council considered ways and means to curb unruly men who were fishing and trading illegally along the New England Coast, and were robbing and antagonizing the Indians.

The 'minutes' show that David Thomson was given assignments at these meetings of the Council, often involving collecting 'dues' from various noble Council members. He seems to have been fairly successful.

One day when David Thomson was in London in the summer or fall of 1622, Seaman William Trevour (Trevore) sought audience with him. Two years earlier, Londoner Trevour had been hired to serve the Brownist pilgrims for one year in

David Thomson: First Yankee

America. Trevour had sailed on the *Mayflower* to New Plymouth with the emigrants. After his year stint in New England, Trevour returned to London on the pilgrim supply ship *Fortune*.

Trevour wished to tell David Thomson of an event which had occurred in America in September 1621. Trevour, Miles Standish, eight other Englishmen and three Indians, including Squanto (Tasquantum) had sailed from New Plymouth is a shallop to explore Massachusetts Bay. They stopped at the island which Thomson had told Miles Standish about when the *Mayflower* was in Plymouth, England, September 1620. It was the island on which Thomson expected to establish a trading post. Squanto positively identified the island telling the group that he, Thomson, and Captain Thomas Dermer were on it together in 1619 when Thomson had spoken of his plan for the island.

Trevour told Thomson that he had suggested to the Pilgrim exploring party on the island that they should take possession of the island in the name of David Thomson. Standish had remonstrated that such action would be a meaningless gesture. Standish named the island, Island Trevour. Trevour said he would like to take possession for Thomson anyway. It could do no harm. Trevour then made a proclamation appropriate to the occasion on September 19, 1621.

Trevour hoped his action would be helpful to Thomson. Thomson thanked Trevour for his thoughtfulness.

David told Sir Ferdinando about Trevour's action in Massachusetts Bay. Gorges laughed, but said, "Good enough. You have wanted that island. We will just include it in the patent which we are writing for you for land at Pascataway."

A reason for Thomson going to London in the fall of 1622 was to secure his promised patent for land in New England so he could get with his preparations to go to Pascataway. The last item in the Council for New England 'minutes' for Saturday,

David Thomson: First Yankee

November 16 reads, "Mr., Thomson's patent was this day signed by the above said Council."

The minutes for the meeting of the Council two weeks later, December 2, 1622, had this entry: "Mr. Thomson propoundeth to have order from ye Council for transportation of ten persons with provisions for New England and the persons so transported to pay the Council the usual rate for their transportation after the expiration of two years." It is noteworthy to observe that whereas all other entries in the 'minutes' talk of transportation of men, this entry referring to David Thomson's expedition refers to the transportation of persons. We infer that some of these indentured servants were to be women. We also infer that these ten persons were indentured to the Council for New England under the direction of David Thomson, agent for the Council for New England.

At the December 3 meeting also, the 'clerks' is directed to get commission forms printed and "It is ordered that Mr. Treasurer can ye seal with him into ye Country, and contract with ye merchants as the commission, given him appeareth , and to give commissions to ye merchants to go on fishing voyages."

It does not appear anywhere in the 'minutes' of the Council for New England, but before David Thomson left London for Plymouth in December 1622, Sir Ferdinando must have informed David Thomson of another responsibility that would soon be placed on him by the Council for New England.

In a patent to Robert Gorges, Sir Ferdinando's son, signed by six Council for New England councilmen (not including Sir Ferdinando) on December 30, 1622 for three hundred square miles of land on the northeast side of Massachusetts Bay, is this clause:

"*...And lastly know ye, that we the said Council have deputed, authorized and appointed, and in our place and stead have put David*

David Thomson: First Yankee

Thomson, Gent., or in his absence any other person that shall be their Governor, or other officer unto the said Council...to be our true and lawful attorney...and in our names to take seisin thereof...and deliver the same to Robert Gorges..." (Gorges: Narration)

Perhaps because of his son's censure by the Lords under date of November 20 for his rash action of presuming to arrest a respected justice of the peace, Sir Ferdinando thought it advisable to get Robert out of the country until the scandal blew over. David Thomson was now to be acting governor of New England until young Gorges could arrive and take over.

Robert Gorges' patent document is the first instance where the term, 'Gent.,' was applied to David Thomson's name. This may not be significant. However, since three of the six signers of the patent were members of the King's Privy Council, it is possible that the appointment and designation indicate that David Thomson was highly respected.

Winter 1622/23: The Thomson's in Plymouth and En Route to Pascataway

A happy reunion awaited David at his home in Plymouth in early December 1622. Amias now looked forward to the time when she would no longer have to endure long separations from her husband. Although there would be hardships in America, at least she would have her husband by her side.

David met with his merchant friends to complete the drafting of the contract for their five year joint enterprise in New England. It was signed by the parties in Plymouth December 14, 1622.

The indenture provided that the merchants would pay eighty-two percent and Thomson eighteen percent of the cost of

David Thomson: First Yankee

sending seven men and their supplies to new England on the Plymouth merchants' ships *Jonathan* and *Providence* in the winter of 1622-1623. On their arrival in New England, Thomson was to supervise the seven men in erecting houses or buildings for habitations.

The first contingent of the Thomson expedition to expand the settlement at Pascataway departed Plymouth on the *Jonathan* in January 1623. In the party were Mr. and Mrs. Thomson and their son John; four or five servants, male and female; and four of the seven men who were to build habitations for fishermen at the fishing station at Pascataway Harbor. Other fishing ships, including Pomeroy's *Providence*, would soon follow with hired and indentured personnel and material bound for the settlement at Pascataway. The ocean crossing was arduous but uneventful.

The *Jonathan* arrived at the Isles of Shoals in early March, 1623, and dropped off some fishermen to join their colleagues who were already on the job after having spent the winter at Pannaway Fort. The *Jonathan* then proceeded to Pascataway where personnel and material were unloaded for Pannaway and the fishing station at the big harbor.

The Thomson party was greeted by natives and white friends at Pannaway. Messages from home were eagerly received by the residents, as were the reports on progress at Pannaway. During the winter a store of beaver skins and other pelts had been accumulated by trading with Indians. There had been no serious illnesses.

Baggage, supplies and equipment were soon carried to the fort and stowed. Personnel were assigned to their billets. Work was started, or continued, on building a barracks and a blacksmith shop. The garden and orchard were expanded. The neighboring Indian tribes were urged to bring their furs to Pannaway.

David Thomson: First Yankee

Fish was plentiful for the settlers. A hunter was designated to keep the settlement supplied with meat.

Not long after their arrival, David Thomson and the four house-builders sailed over to Pascataway Harbor in a shallop. They selected sites for building log habitations for Plymouth fishermen next winter. A few weeks later they were joined by the other three men who had arrived from Plymouth on the *Providence*. The seven men spent the spring, summer and fall of 1623 building cabins and other structures for the little fishing village at Pascataway. They made a couple of fishing stages, drying racks, and a storage shed so that fish processing could be performed at the Big Harbor as well as at the Isle of Shoals.

Thomson announced to the community that before he had left Plymouth he had received a message from Sir Ferdinando Gorges to the effect that Sir Ferdinando's son, Robert, with whom some of the settlers were acquainted, was to come to New England in the summer with a large group of colonists to start a settlement on the northeast shore of Massachusetts Bay, where Robert had been awarded a patent for thirty square miles of land. Young Gorges was to be the Governor of New England. He would establish a government for the colony. The government would include a parliament. Hopefully, in a year or two, Sir Ferdinando would come over and be the governor. Perhaps he would occupy Fort Pannaway. In the meantime, David Thomson had been designated as the agent for the Council for New England and as deputy for Robert Gorges until the Governor arrived on the scene. Thomson also announced that, when he could, he planned to move to his island in Massachusetts Bay for which he had a patent. There he would set up a trading post. He would also maintain his partnership with the Plymouth merchants for fishing and trading around Pascataway and the Isles of Shoals.

David Thomson: First Yankee

Fishing Station at Pascataway Harbor

By 1623, there was no more room on the Isles of Shoals for additional fishing stages, so Plymouth fishermen set up fish processing facilities at Pascataway Harbor on Great Island near their plantation.

Fishing was done by crews of three men working from shallops propelled with a single sail or oars. A boat could carry a ton of fish. Fish were caught by net, seine or hook. When a load of fish was caught, the shallop usually proceeded to the fishing station at the Isles of Shoals or Pascataway Harbor. The boats pulled alongside of a fishing stage which was a raft or float moored off shore and connected to the land with a floating walk way. The platform and walkway sections were buoyed by logs fastened together side by side. A fishing stage had a bin big enough to hold two tons of fish. It had a large operating table with work space enough for half a dozen men.

The fish were unloaded from the shallop in to the bin. The shallop returned to the sea to get another load. The shore-based processors working at the stage table beheaded, slit, gutted and split the fish. Resulting fish flakes (slabs) were tossed into baskets or tote barrows to be carried ashore to drying racks or salting sheds. The refuse from the fish was dumped into the water.

Plymouth ships called at the Isles of shoals and Pascataway in June and December each year at the ends of the spring and fall fishing seasons. They brought mail, personnel and supplies from Plymouth. They loaded the readied fish and took them to markets in England, the continent and the Mediterranean. They also carried messages, personnel and produce back to England.

The following section is a verbatim excerpt from Notes on the First Planting of New Hampshire, by John S. Jeness,

David Thomson: First Yankee

published in 1895. It gives a colorful description of Pannaway in 1623-1624.

"Pannaway plantation became at once well known along the New England coast and was visited within its very first year by many of the most interesting and striking characters connected with our early history. Phinehas Pratt came there as early as may, 1623, and before the great crackling fires of a cold spring, recounted, no doubt, the story of the terrible winter he had passed at Wessaguscus; of his marvelous escape from the murderous savages across a trackless frozen forest for near fifty miles into the New Plymouth in quiet of succor, and of the valiant achievements of the redoubtable Miles Standish, who, with a small and of soldiers, set out the very next day from the Pilgrim village, and slaying Pecksuot, the savage chief, with his own hand, succeeded in dispersing the Indians and rescuing the trembling, exhausted planters of Wesaguscus from impending annihilation.

A month or two later, came into Pannaway a half drowned, half naked man, imploring succor and protection. He proved to me Mr. Thomas Weston, the faithful friend and agent of the Pilgrim fathers in England before they sailed away for the new world, though at present they entertained toward him sentiments of distrust and unkindliness. His political and religious sentiments did not accord with those of the separatists at New Plymouth. Weston had now been cast away, while cruising along the New Hampshire coast between Boar's Head and Merrimack river; his shallop wrecked, and himself afterwards assailed and stripped of his clothes by the Indians. The miserable man succeeded at last, however, in making his way along the coast into Pannaway, and there he was clad and restored to health and furnished with means to return to Plymouth.

David Thomson: First Yankee

About this same time, the Pilgrim hero, Miles Standish himself, made his appearance at Pannaway. "Standish," says Hubbard, "had been bred a soldier in the low counties and never entered the school of Christ or of John the Baptist, or if ever he was there, he had forgot his first lessons. A little chimney is soon fired, so was the Plymouth captain, a man of very small stature yet of a very hot and angry temper. The valiant captain, at the conclusion of his stout achievements in the rescue of Wessaguscus, was employed to buy provisions at the eastward "for the refreshing of the Plymouth colony." He must have been at Pannaway about the last of June, as he returned to Plymouth in July laden with provisions he was in quest of, and bringing along in his company our Mr. David Thomson from Pannaway.

That the Indians were visitors at Pannaway during the very first years of its foundation, appears from the narrative of Phineas Pratt, who wrote that "at the time of his (Levett) being at Pacataway a sachem or Sagamor gave two of his men, one to Captain Levett and another to Mr. Thomson:" but one that was there said, "How can you trust those savages? Call the name of one 'Watt Tyler' and the other 'Jack Straw,' after the names of the two greatest Rebills et ever were in England."

Neither was the society of women wholly lacking at Pannaway during this period. David Thomson's wife resided with him at his new plantation, and it is reasonable to believe that she came not without female companions." (end quote)

Four year old John Thomson was the only English child at Pannaway in 1623. He received a lot of attention. The Indians had never seen a little white boy. They came from miles around to see what he looked like.

John was an adventurous child, and the Indian slave, Watt Tyler, was given the responsibility of knowing where John was at all times. John very quickly picked up the local Indian dialect.

David Thomson: First Yankee

John later became a master mariner and was captain of his own ship before he was 30.

In December 1623, Thomas Weston's vessel, the Swan, arrived at Pannaway. On board was the Governor-General, Captain Robert Gorges. Thomson had known Robert Gorges since they were small children, and had been acting as his official representative at Pannaway.

Robert Gorges expedition had met unexpected difficulties. A late arrival in Massachusetts Bay had left them ill prepared for the winter. The shacks that existed at Wessagusset were unfit for a man of the Governor's position. Their supply ship had not arrived. It was doubtful if their current stores would last the winter. Therefore, Robert had decided that his party should spend the winter at his father's fort in Pascataway. The arrangement with Weston was that his pinnace would transport the Governor and his party to Pannaway in return for enough supplies to carry Weston and his crew to Virginia.

Georges said there might be as many as twenty of his people to spend the winter at Pannaway. Some might return to Virginia with Weston, some wanted to return to England if that were possible.

Thomson explained that Pannaway was taking care of some refugees from the original Wessagusset settlement and that an addition of twenty more souls would put a strain on Pannaway resources during the winter. However, with Thomson in complete charge of the commissary, and with moderate austerity practices, the community could probably get through the winter. Thomson also requested the authority to require the assistance of any person in the community, persons of quality excepted. Governor Gorges agreed.

Three weeks later, a Plymouth fishing vessel arrived from England via the Isles of Shoals where it had loaded processed

David Thomson: First Yankee

fish of the fall season catch. Captain Christopher Levett was a passenger. Levett and his baggage were lightened ashore at Pannaway. The the ship proceeded to its destination at the fishing station at Pacattaway Harbor, two miles up river.

Levett was an officer in the royal navy, in high favor at court, and much distinguished in the old country. Levett had come to New England with a patent from the Council for New England which permitted him to choose 6000 acres of land in New England. His indentured men had been transported earlier and were now probably at Mohegan Island or Casco Bay. Before disembarking, Levett requested the master of the fishing vessel which transported him to get word to his men down east to assemble at Pannaway as soon as possible.

Captain Levett spent roughly a month at Pannaway, during which time he met with Governor Gorges, who told him that he was joined with him in commission as a counsellor. There was a great ceremony at Pannaway to install Levett as a member of the Council for New England.

Levett brought three items of disconcerting news. He said that the opposition to the Council of New England's authority to regulate fishing was increasing. He also told that the threat of war with Spain was increasing and that the King might have to reconvene parliament in order to get funds. And lastly, he told Governor Gorges that his young friends who were supposed to send supplies for the new settlement at Massachusetts Bay had not done anything about it up to the time Levett left England. There seemed to be no leadership or feeling of responsibility manifest among the young men.

At the end of January, 1624, Levett departed Pannaway with eleven men in two boats to explore northeastward to find a suitable place for him to start a plantation which he intended to call "York."

David Thomson: First Yankee

Though a few of Gorges group may have returned to England on the ship that had brought Levett to Pannaway, Robert Gorges and several others spent the remainder of the winter. Some were discouraged, but others were eager to give settlement in New England a further try.

Meanwhile in England, Sir Fernando Gorges was still trying to win financial support from Western England fishing interests for his plans to establish permanent settlements in New England. Gorges sought to have the king use his power and influence with the fishermen. The fishermen wanted the king to withdraw the Charter of New England. The king was reluctant to get involved. The fishing interests waited for Parliament to be reconvened when and where they could re-open the fight for free fishing. Sir Fernando's supporters were disheartened but the valiant Knight fought on.

Parliament opened on February 23, 1634. On the second day of business, a bill for free fishing was introduced and immediately assigned to the Committee on Grievance for fast action. If tax on fishing was determined to be a "Grievance," then the grievance would automatically be discontinued.

Gorges defended his charter, with its fish control clause, before Parliament, but lost. In March, Gorges agreed to permit free fishing in order to save the rest of the charter. Sometime in May, the word that fishing was free reached New England. The people of Pannaway also learned that war with Spain was imminent. For young Governor Gorges, everything was lost. Without financial support, he could do nothing in the New World. Besides, he was a soldier whose place was with the military in England.

David Thomson: First Yankee

Massachusetts 1624-1628

When Governor-General Robert Gorges' plantation on Massachusetts Bay failed in 1623, he appointed 21-year-old Samuel Maverick to look after his property there. At the same time, he appointed David Thomson to be his chief agent for the Council for New England in America, and to serve as deputy governor until a replaced. Gorges directed David Thomson to construct a fortified headquarters for Maverick on Gorges property in Massachusetts Bay, employing the crew of builders who were indentured to the Council for New England and residing in Pannaway He also directed that some cannon from Pannaway Fort be moved to arm Maverick's house.

The departing governor requested that Thomson assist members of Gorges party who chose to stay in America. He suggested that these people settle in Massachusetts Bay, but NOT on Gorges' land. He promised that he would support their claim for squatter's rights with his father and the Council for any sites on which they might settle, providing they were not on his grant.

Governor Gorges desired to consult with Captain Levett before he returned to England. Levett had been commissioned as a member of the Governors' Council at Pannaway in December. In January, he had started to explore the Maine coast to find a location for his 6000 acre patent. He chose a place on Casco Bay.

Thomson arranged transport for Gorges to Casco Bay. Gorges took with him from the Pannaway arsenal two pieces of ordinance and ammunition, to arm Levett's house.

At Casco, Levett had learned he could not expect support from England. He decided he might just as well return home and take his place in the navy where he belonged.

David Thomson: First Yankee

Sometime in June, 1924, Gorges and Levett sailed from Casco Bay on a vessel returning to England with a cargo of fish, leaving a garrison of ten men to look after Levett's place. A few years later, Levett's propery was sold to "Mr. Creely, Mr. Jop, and Company" of Plymouth. Jop and Creely were merchants and friends of David and Amais Thomson.

People at Pannaway passed the following winter comfortably enough. Food supply had been adequate. Fuel for fires was plentiful. Trading with the Indians had continued and there was a supply of furs to send back to England. David had accumulated a few excellent masts to send back to his shipwright father-in-law in Plymouth. Clearing for gardens and orchards continued, and the building of boats was entered upon.

A few men, whose indentured obligations with the Council were completed, signed on as fisherman and fished during the spring season.

When word had reached Pannaway that the war with Spain was inevitable, the defense preparations at the fort were reviewed. Defense duty stations were assigned, and an alarm system was set up in case of threat from sea or land, or from red or white foe. Pannaway was well-armed and provided with ammunition. Some of the men who had worked with David at the Fort in England were familiar with heavy ordinance. They were assigned to duty as Cannoneers.

After Governor Gorges left Pannaway (about June 1, 1624) to go to Casco Bay to consult with Captain Levett and then return to England, David Thomson organized an expedition to Massachusetts Bay to carry out his assignments there. He took with him men who were indentured to the Council for New England. Many were builders who had worked with him at Plymouth and Pannaway forts.

The first task was to build the fortified house for Samuel

David Thomson: First Yankee

Maverick. Maverick, in his *Description of New England* (1660), had this to say about his home:

> "*Winnisime. Two miles south from Rumney Marsh on the north side of Mistick River is Winnisime which though but a few houses on it, yet deserves to be mentioned. One home is yet standing there which is the Antientest house in the Massachusetts Government, a house which in the year 1625 I fortified with a pillizado and flankers and guns both below and above in them which awed the Indians who at that time had a mind to cut off the English. They once faced it but receiving a repulse never attempted it more although (as they now confess) the repent it when about 2 years after they say so many English come over.*"

We glean from Maverick's use of the word 'Antientest' that his house was the first one built on Boston Bay. We note that Maverick says he fortified his house in 1625, which is a little different from saying that he built it in 1625. Maverick was not a builder. David Thomson and his crew were the builders. It is reasonable to assume that the construction of Winnisime was started in 1624 by David Thomson and that the arming of it took place in 1625. The guns must have come from the Pannaway arsenal.

William Hilton visited with David Thomson when he was building Winnisime. Hilton requested help in getting his family to Pascattaway where his brother, Edward Hilton, was a fisherman. Edward had come to Pascattaway with Thomson in 1621. Thomson made the arrangements and the Hiltons move to Pannaway and then to Pascattaway Harbor. Four years later the Hilton brothers started a settlement at Hilton's Point (Dover) and received a land patent from the Council for New England.

Edmund Johnson came to Massachusetts Bay in June 1630 with the first ('great migration') Puritans to settle there. Johnson (*Wonder-Working Providence*) also commented on Winnisime.

David Thomson: First Yankee

"...where Mr. Samuel Maverick then living...had built a small fort with the help of one Mr. David Thomson, placing four murtherers [cannon] to protect him from the Indians." "...near an island called Thomson's Island lived some few planters more. These persons were the first planters of those parts having some small trading with the Indians for beaver skins."

Others of Governor Robert Gorges' group settled on Massachusetts Bay in 1624. They were William Jeffrey, John Burslem, William Blackstone, John Balch and Thomas Walford. Some of them had family and servants. David Thomson built his home on Thompson's Island in 1625 but did not move his family there until 1626. Only Maverick of this group of old planters lived on Robert Gorges' land grant.

Winnisime - Samuel Maverick's home - 1625
"The Antientest house in Massachusetts Bay
                              Matthew R. Thompson III

David Thomson: First Yankee

Wimmisime became the social, commercial and defense center for the scattered community on Massachusetts Bay. Communication with England was maintained through Pascataway, where fishing ships of Plymouth merchants regularly operated. Such furs as the Bay settlers procured were delivered to Maverick who passed them on to Thomson, who sent them to England.

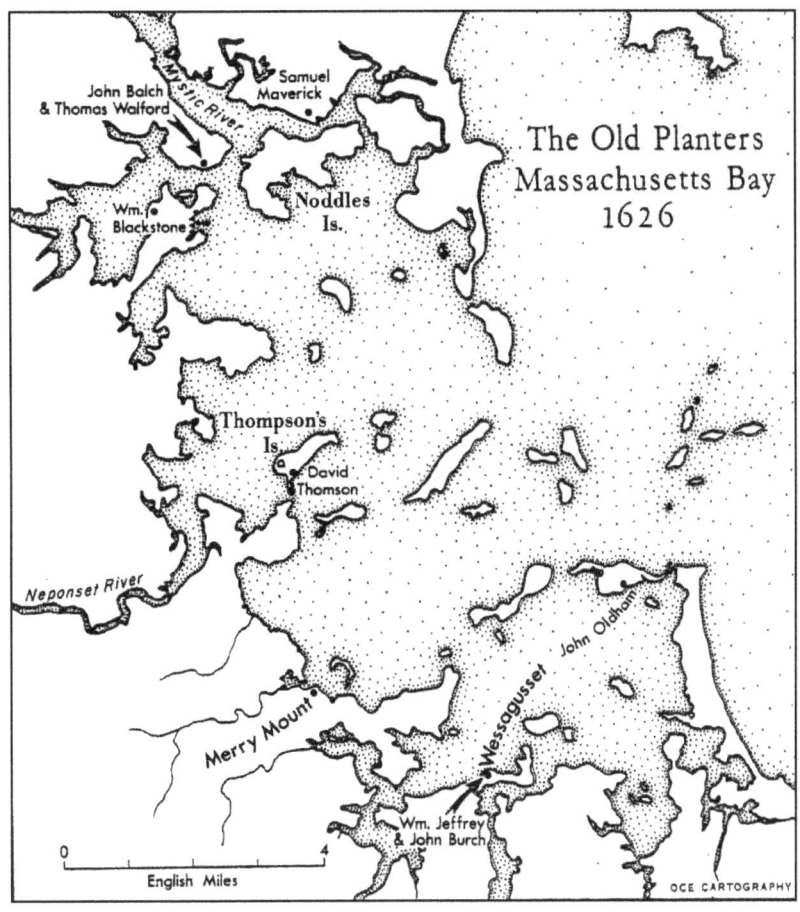

David Thomson: First Yankee

David Thomson's Home and Trading Port

Bradley: *Island School History*, has this description of David Thomson's house on Thompson's Island:

"He (Thomson) located his house on the bank, on the east shore just south of the center of the island. The house like most of the early houses, was set by the four points of the compass facing the south. It was probably twenty-five or thirty feet square, or nearly so, one story high and built of logs. The roof, built of logs covered either with thatch or clay and mud, was very steep. The single door was in the center of the south side, and there was a window on each of the other sides of the house. Inside was a large room, at the back of which stood the broad and deep fireplace four feet across, which served both for cooking and for warmth. The hearth was large with capacious ingles for seats from which gleamed the sky overhead. The cellar walls as well as the chimney were built of large rough field stone, and the cellar floor was laid with bricks ten inches square, which must have come from England by way of Little Harbor."

"In 1889, while digging on the east bank, the ruins of the old cellar walls and chimney were discovered. They were well preserved after being covered with six feet of soil for two hundred years. They ocean had, evidently, worn the bank away for many feet, for only the west corner, part of the wet and north walls, with the base of the chimney, and part of the cellar floor remained intact. All the rest of the cellar had yielded to the influence of the water and wind. The west corner is formed by two stone walls about ten feet long by six feet deep, irregular both at the top and at the southern exposure. Evidently, the east and south walls had fallen over the face of the bank. The remains of the large, open fireplace were found at the back built into the bank. Among these ruins the bowls and stems of long Dutch pipes were unearthed."

David Thomson: First Yankee

Pannaway and Pascattaway

1625 marked a changed in the status of David Thomson's Pannaway colony. At the start of the year, the settlers were unsure where they stood. By the end of the year, they knew they were on their own.

The most active men on the Council for New England, including Gorges, became completely involved in the war with Spain. The colonists could expect no guidance or support from the Council. However, trade with Plymouth continued, with fishing ships regularly making round trips, twice per year, between England and the Isles of Shoals.

Additional fishing facilities were built along the east side of Great Island. The number of permanent personnel there increased, and some families were brought over from England to be with their men.

As the terms of indentured service to the Council for New England were fulfilled by men who had come to Pannaway in 1621 and 1623, most elected to stay in New England. Some continued to work for Thomson under various arrangements. Many continued to fish, trapping or trading in the off season.

The war did not come to New England. It was not expected to, but the people of the community cooperated to maintain their guard. At any threat from land or sea, from Indian or European foe, the members of the community could repair to Pannaway. An assault never came.

Those people who bought or leased land from David Thomson chose not to have their homesites on Great Island, because it was understood that the 600 acre island would eventually belong to the Plymouth merchants. Instead they picked plots around Pannaway, Little Harbor, or Strawbery Banke.

David Thomson: First Yankee

Trading Goods

During the spring of 1626, Thomson learned that the trading post at Mohegan Island was going to go out of business and that there was a stock of trading goods to be disposed of. Soon thereafter the Pilgrims at New Plymouth had the same information. Governor Bradford decided he would go to Monhegan and buy what he could. The following is an excerpt from his book, *Of Plymouth Plantation*:

"And wanting trading goods, they understood that a plantation which was at Mohegan and belonged to some merchants of Plymouth, was to break up and divers useful goods were there to be sold. The Governor and Mr. Winslow took a boat and some hands and went higher. But Mr. David Thomson, who lived at Piscataqua, understanding their purpose, took opportunity to go with them, which was some hindrance to them both. For they, perceiving their joint desires to buy, held their goods at higher rates, and not only so, but would not sell a parcel of their trading goods except they sold all. So lest they should further prejudice one another, they agreed to buy all and divide them equally between them. They bought also a parcel of goats which they distributed at home as they saw need and occasion, and took corn for them of the people, which gave them good content, their moiety of the goods came to above 400 pounds sterling."

Not only were the Pilgrims well furnished for trade, but so was Thomson. He was amply supplied for both of his trading posts, the one at Pannaway and the other on Thomson's Island.

During the early summer of 1926, Thomson moved his family from Pannaway Fort to their new home on Thomson's Island. At this time, David was 33 years old, Amias was 28 and John was seven. A few servants were taken along to help Amias

David Thomson: First Yankee

take care of the livestock, garden and outside chores; as well as to assist David with the trading post when necessary.

It was not difficult for Thomson to look after his business at both Massachusetts Bay and Pascataway. When wind and weather were favorable it was an easy day's sail.

The Death of David Thomson

The time, place and manner of David Thomson's death are not known. Historians suppose that Thomson died not later than early June, 1628, when Mrs. Thomson made a recorded contribution in her own name. The presumption is that she must have been a widow when she did that.

There is not the slightest clue as to how David Thomson died, though if Thomson had been murdered, or slain by Indians in an uprising, it would likely have appeared in some record.

Amias Cole Thomson-Maverick

Amias (Cole) Thomson-Maverick was a bystander or participant in more facets of early New England history than any other woman. Daughter of a Plymouth shipwright, she seems to have been popular with the guildsmen merchants who ran the city and who sent their fish ships to New England from the earliest days. Sketchy records suggest that Amias was the 25th English woman to migrate to New England. Preceding her were the twenty women on the *Mayflower* (1620), thirteen of whom died the first year. Four more women went to New Plimouth on the *Fortune* in 1621. Amias arrived at Pascataway on the *Jonathan* in the late winter of 1623.

David Thomson: First Yankee

David and Amias Thomson entertained almost everybody of consequence at Pascataway during her first year there. Amongst them was Thomas Weston, Captain Miles Standish, Phineas Pratt, Governor Robert Gorges and most of his would-be settlers including Samuel Maverick and Captain Christopher Levett. Indians were also visitors at Pascataway. William Hilton and his family were probably entertained there in 1624 after being pushed out of New Plimouth.

The Thomsons moved to their island home in Massachusetts Bay in 1626. It was the center of social life of the Old Planters. Soon after David Thomson died in 1628, Amias married Samuel Maverick and went to live with him at Winnisime.

In June 1630, the Mavericks entertained at Winnisime Governor John Winthrop and members of the first contingent of Puritans to arrive in Boston Harbor.

On August 16, 1631, three men were fined by the Massachusetts authorities for "abusing themselves disorderly with drinking too much strong drink...at Mr. Maverick his house..." The incident may or may not have indicated Maverick hospitality but it does suggest a conviviality in contrast to the grim and forbidding mien of the Puritans. It marks the beginning of the life-long tension between Church of England loyalist Samuel Maverick and the separatist puritanical Puritans.

An example of Amias' courage and character was in connection with the smallpox epidemic which killed so many Indians in 1633. Winthrop in his *Journal* wrote: "Among others, Mr. Maverick of Winnissime is worthy of perpetual remembrance. Himself, his wife, and servants, went daily to them (the Indians), ministered to their necessities and buried their dead, and took home nay of their children." The Mavericks were said to have buried some thirty Indians in one day.

David Thomson: First Yankee

Maverick acquired Noddle's Island in April, 1633. He built a house on that island in 1634. The Mavericks were residing on Noddle's Island in 1635. In March 1635, Maverick was ordered to move to Boston by the Puritan authorities. He was ordered to refrain from entertaining strangers. The Puritan authorities obviously considered the warm hospitality the Mavericks accorded to 'strangers' to be a subversive influence on the Puritan view that life should be grim and dour. Instead of complying, Maverick moved his father and mother, Reverend John and Mary (Gye) Maverick of Dorchester, into his Noddle's Island home and took off for Virginia to get some corn. He remained there nearly a year. Father John died (February, 1636) during son Samuel's absence. Amais had her hands full taking care of her own three Maverick children, Nathaniel, Samuel Jr., and Mary as well as her in-laws. Amias' widowed mother-in-law was to remain in the Samuel Maverick household for thirty years.

Winthrop records Maverick's return to Boston on August 3, 1636- "Samuel Maverick, who had been in Virginia near twelve months, now returned with two pinnaces, and brought some 14 heifers, and about 80 goats." He also brought "ten niggers."

Samuel and Amias Maverick were becoming wealthy from Samuel's far flung trading activities around the Atlantic rim. They had a considerable ménage on Noddle's Island, possibly including Negro slaves. They continued to be hospitable "to persons of all sorts." Some instances are reported as follows:

In July 1637, the Mavericks entertained Sir Henry Vane and Lord Ley.

John Joselyn, in his *Voyages to New England*, wrote of Maverick that, in the summer of 1638, he went ashore upon Noddle's Island to Mr. Samuel Maverick "...the only hospitable man in all the country, giving entertainment to all strangers."

David Thomson: First Yankee

Joselyn returned to Noddle's Island after a couple of months. He wrote about his welcome as follows: "...I was come to Maverick's he would not let me go aboard no more until the ship was ready to sail."

Three incidents illustrate the strength of character and independence of Amias Thomson-Maverick:

1. The Thomson's Island trading post and home was the economic and social center of the Massachusetts Bay residents in 1628 when David Thomson died. Widow Amias was immediately confronted with the decision of whether she should contribute to the cost of exporting Thomas Morton to England for trial. In the list of the seven contributors to the fund is one woman, -Mrs. Thomson, fifteen shillings. The Pilgrim colony at New Plymouth contributed fifty shillings as did the Pascataway fishing village. They were the largest contributors.

2. During the period while Maverick was in Virginia in 1635-1636, Amias wrote a letter to her friend, Robert Trelawney. Trelawney had been Mayor of Plymouth, England, in 1633. His father was Mayor when Robert, Amias Cole and David Thomson were youngsters together in Plymouth. The letter gives a clue to Amias character showing that she was not one to relinquish a valuable asset meekly.

3. May 26, 1648, Amias had public notary William Aspinwall record the "Collee-Thomson Marriage Settlement" in which her father, William Cole, Plymouth shipwright, granted David Thomson, Apothecary, and his wife Ems (Amias) a house "near the old conduit" in Plymouth. The date of the marriage settlement was April 1, 1615.

A supplement to the marriage settlement dated January 3, 1625/6 was recorded at the same time, in which William Cole, shipwright, acknowledged he had received of his "daughter, Amias Thomson, the sum of fifty pounds which I was to have towards buying my land." Cole also acknowledged receipt of thirty pounds turned over to him to invest for Amias and her husband.

The letter from Mrs. Amias Maverick to Robert Trelawney was printed in <u>Trelawney Papers</u> in Volume III of <u>Maine Historical Society, Second Series.</u> Portland, Maine, 1884.

Notells Island in Massachusetts Bay
The 20th of November, 1635

Good Sir: I kindly salute you in the Lord. I am given to understand by divers that my father is verie much incensed against me, but by what meanes I know not, and that he hath offered to make sale of his land, notwithstanding he convenye it to me by his deed (which I doubt not but will prove sufficient), and had of me fifty pounds in consideration of it, that so the land might remaine to me & my children after my ffathers decease. And now I am enformed that my ffather would fayne dispose of the land & repay this fifty pounds. Now my humble request unto your worship is, that as you loved my first husband, so you would be pleased to doe that favor for me and my ffatherless children as to speake to my father concerning this thing, for I am perswaded your good word to his in our behalf will much prevail, and wheras my father (as I am told) would dispose of the land and have mee to take the fifty pounds againe, I shall desire you to intreate him that it may remaine with him, for my children, & he would not goe about to putt the land from us contrary to his deeds & promises. As for the house which I lived in, my father gave it me presently in marriage, and I have left it wholy to his disposeing since I came thence, without having any benefit of it, only to give my father content. And thus craving

David Thomson: First Yankee

pardon for my greate boldness, not doubting but that you will be pleased to doe me this favour, whein both I and mine shall ever rest obliged unto you, and thus with my best respects to your selfe & your loving wife, I humbly take my leave, and reamine, your friend.

AMIAS MAVERICKE

I shall intreate you to remember me kindly to Mr. Clemett.

  To the worshipfull and my much respected friend, Mr. Robert Trelawney, merchant, give these, in Plymouth. Per the way of Bristoll.

Amias' action in recording these documents indicates unusual business sense for a woman of that era. That she was able to send thirty pounds to her father to invest in 1626 indicates that the Thomsons were prospering. Thirty pounds was three times the annual income of a skilled workman.

  The Mavericks lived at Noddle's Island from 1634 to 1650. Amias kept house for Samuel and his mother, and for their three Maverick children, -Nathaniel, Samuel and Mary born about 1630, 1632 and 1635, respectively. Amias' son, John Thomson, started his apprentice seamen training in 1633 and was seldom home. Daughter, Prissilla Thomson, remained in Plymouth with her grandparents.

  During this period, Mr. Maverick was often at odds with the Puritan authorities who were working to establish a Puritan church-centered government. Maverick held out for reasonable rights for non-Puritans. He was imprisoned and fined several times for his views and actions.

David Thomson: First Yankee

About 1651, the Mavericks moved to Saco, Maine. Here, again, Samuel Maverick became at odds with the Massachusetts Puritans who claimed that their charter gave them New Hampshire and Maine as well as parts of Rhode Island and Connecticut.

About 1660, Maverick was sent to London as a delegate of other non-Puritans to try to induce the crown to curb the oppressive New England Puritan government. During his four years in London, Maverick won considerable support for his views. It was while he was in London that he wrote his invaluable *Description of New England*. He presented it to Sir Edward Hyde, Earl of Clarendon, Charles II's Lord High Chancellor. Among the many (undated) letters which Maverick wrote to the Earl of Clarendon is one which concisely states his case against the Massachusetts Puritan Government:

Right Honorable

May it please your lordship if I misunderstood you not, you ordered me to draw up the heads of what might be thought requisite for those of the Massachusetts to condescend unto, upon the Continuation of the Charter. I most humbly conceive they may be such as these following.

That all freeholders may have votes in election of officers civil and military. [Only puritan church members were allowed to vote.]

That all persons inoffensive in life and conversation may be admitted to the sacrament of the Lord's Supper and their children to Baptism. [Such rights were forbidden in New England even for Church of England members.]

That such laws as are now in force there, derogating from the laws of England may be repealed. [English laws permitted relative freedom of religion. Puritan laws did not.]

That the oath of Allegiance may be administered instead of that which they term the oath of fidelity. [Puritan required their church members to swear allegiance to the Massachusetts government and forswear the king. Maverick wanted the settlers to swear allegiance to the King.]

That they go not beyond their just bounds, even those which for near twenty years they were content withal. [Stop encroaching on neighboring colonies.]

That they admit of appeals on just and reasonable grounds.

That they permit such as desire it, to use ye common prayer.

That all writs may be issued out in his Majesty's name.

My Lord I hope you are persuaded of the great necessity there is of sending over some commissioners for the further and better settling of these colonies, now out of order. I most humbly beseech you that all convenient expedition may be made, the summer passing fast away.

As for the Dutch I have presumed to give your Lord notice, how they encroach and increase and what course they have taken to invite people to them [New Amsterdam], and how several of our English families are going to them. I leave all to your Lords most wise consideration, and shall always attend your commands, remaining you Lord's most humble servant, Samuel Maverick.

To the right Honorable Edward, Earle of Clarendon L. high Chancellor of England be these most humbly presented. (Clarendon Papers)

In 1664, Samuel Maverick and three other men were appointed Commissioners to go to New England and carry out the idea in the above letter. They were not successful with the Massachusetts government. However, they did bring New Amsterdam [New York] under the English Crown with no bloodshed and with a minimum of disruption. For his part in the latter project, Maverick was given a house on lower Broadway, New York City. Presumably, this is where Samuel and Amias

David Thomson: First Yankee

Maverick died in the 1670's.

Amias (Cole) Thomson-Maverick (1597-1670+) was in the thick of things regarding New England during her entire life; first in Plymouth, England; then in New Hampshire, Massachusetts and Maine; and finally in New York. Would that some person would write an imaginative story of her life.

BIBLIOGRAPHY

Barbour: Pocahontas. Philip L. Barbour: Pocahontas and her World; Houghton Mifflin; Boston 1970

Baxter: Gorges. James Phinney Baxter, "Sir Ferdinando Gorges and his Province of Maine", Prince Society. Boston, 1890

Bracken: Plymouth. C. W. Bracken: A History of Plymouth and Her Neighbors. Plymouth, England, 1931, 1970.

Bradford: History. William Bradford: Of Plymouth Plantation; Boston, 1856. Available in many editions.

Bradford: Letter-Book. William Bradford: "Letter-Book", Mass. Hist. Society, Collections, Ser. I. v. 3-4; Boston, 1794

Brown: Genesis. Alexander Brown, ed; The Genesis of the United States. Houghton-Mifflin, New York, 1891.

Clarendon Papers. New York Hist. Soc. 1869

CNE: Minutes. The Records of the Council for New England. American Antiquarian Society Proceedings; 2nd ser., XXII. Worcester, Mass., 1876 and 1912.

Davies: Relation. James Davies, Navigator: "The relation of a voyage (to Pemaquid, Maine) 1607" Manuscript found in 1875. Published in Mass. Hist. Soc. v. XVIII 1886. Also in Levermore: Forerunners..

Dean: Mason. James Ward Dean, ed: Captain John Mason, the Founder of New Hampshire. Prince Society; Boston, 1887

Deane: Indenture. Charles Deane:"Indenture of David Thomson and Others" Mass. Hist. Soc. Proceedings, v.XIV, 1875-6; Boston, 1876.

Gill:Plymouth. Crispin Gill: Plymouth, A New History, Ice Age to the Elizabethan; David & Charles; Newton Abbot, Devon. 1966.

Gorges: Narration. Sir Ferdinando Gorges: A Briefe Narration of the original undertakings of the advancement of plantations into the parts of America ...., Written ca 1642, published London 1658. Maine Hist. Soc., Ser. I, v II, Portland, 1847

Gorges: Relation. A Briefe Relation of the discovery and plantation of New England ....(1607-1622). London, 1622. printed in Baxter: Gorges.

Jenness: First Planting. John S. Jenness: "Notes on the first planting of New Hampshire and on the Piscataqua patents." N.H. State Papers, v XXV, Town Charters, v II. Concord, 1895

Johnson: Providence. "Wonder Working Providence, 1628-1651," published in Original Narratives of Early American History, J. Franklin James, ed.; v 9. New York, Barnes and Noble, 1910

Levermore: __Forerunners__. Charles Herbert Levermore, ed.: __Forerunners and competitors of the Pilgrims and Puritans__. Two volumes. New England Society of Brooklyn, 1912

Levett: __Voyage__. Christopher Levett: "A voyage into New England begun in 1623 and ended in 1624 performed by Christopher Levett," London, 1628. Published in Maine Hist. Soc. __Collections__, v 2, 1847.

Maverick: __Description__. "A briefe discription of New England and the severall townes therein, together with the present government thereof." NEHGR v XXXIX, Jan. 1885.

Morton: __Canaan__. Thomas Morton: __New English Canaan__. Amsterdam, 1637. Reprinted by the Prince Society, Boston, 1883.

Mourt: __Relation__. (William Bradford and Edward Winslow): __A relation, or Journall, of the Beginnings and Proceedings of the English Plantation settled at Plimoth in New England.__ London, 1622. Reprints.

NEHGR = New England Historic and Genealogical Register, a quarterly published by the society, Boston, since 1847.

Preston: __Gorges__. Richard Arthur Preston: __Gorges of Plymouth Fort__, a life of Sir Ferdinando Gorges, ..., U of Toronto Press; Toronto, 1953.

PRO = Public Record Office. English archives. Chancery Lane, London.

Rosier: __Waymouth's Voyage__. James Rosier: "__A true relation of the most prosperous voyage made this present yeare 1605, by Captain George Waymouth__ ..." Printed in Levermore: __Forerunners__

Smith: __Description__. Captain John Smith: "Description of New England" London, 1616. Many editions published.

Smith: __Trials__. John Smith: __New England's Trials__; London, 1622.

Smith: __History__. John Smith: __General Historie of Virginia__, London, 1624.

Stoneman: __Challons' Voyage__. John Stoneman, pilot: "The voyage of M. Henry Challons intended for the north plantation of Virginia, 1606; taken by the way, and ill used by Spaniards." Published by Samuel Purchas: __His Pilgrimes__, 1625. Reprinted in Brown: __Genesis__.

Willison: __Saints__. George F. Willison: __Saints and Strangers__; being the Lives of the Pilgrim Fathers ..., Reynal & Hitchcock, New York, 1945.

Winslow: __Good Newes__. "Good Newes from New England," London, 1624.

Winthrop: __History__. John Winthrop: __A History of New England from 1630 to 1649.__ Many editions.

Worth: __Plymouth__. R. N. Worth: __History of Plymouth__; Wm Brendon & Son; Plymouth, 1890.

When Barbara Newall was a student at the University of New Hampshire in the 1940s, she could not have predicted where her ties to the school and the New Hampshire Seacoast would lead her decades later.

She is proud to have been a member of the Friends of Odiorne Point Board, which later merged into the Seacoast Science Center, and played a role in building the Center from a seasonal nature center to the year-round marine education center it is today.

Proceeds from this book will benefit the Seacoast Science Center.

www.ingramcontent.com/pod-product-compliance
Lightning Source LLC
Chambersburg PA
CBHW051806040426
42446CB00007B/543